Building Learning Capacity in an Age of Uncertainty

In an increasingly complex context of global pandemic, economic uncertainty, increased racial inequities, and a climate crisis, this practical guide for school leaders explores how capacity as learning at the individual, team, and organizational level can help schools become more agile and adaptive. Author James A. Bailey unpacks a new model of capacity building that combines learning process, leadership mindsets, and skills to enhance learning. This research-based book includes a "Diagnostic for School Learning Capacity" and "Team Considerations" to help school leaders and their teams launch further discussions and advance learning in their contexts. The tools in this timely book are designed to help school leaders handle the increasing volatile, uncertain, complex, and ambiguous world in which schools now exist.

James A. Bailey is a former elementary and high school principal, assistant superintendent, superintendent, and turnaround leader. He is currently a school improvement consultant and leadership coach at Brass Tacks Innovations, and serves as a faculty member at Walden University, USA.

Building Learning Capacity in an Age of Uncertainty

Leading an Agile and Adaptive School

James A. Bailey

NEW YORK AND LONDON

First published 2021
by Routledge
605 Third Avenue, New York, NY 10158

and by Routledge
2 Park Square, Milton Park, Abingdon, Oxon OX14 4RN

Routledge is an imprint of the Taylor & Francis Group, an informa business

© 2021 James A. Bailey

The right of James A. Bailey to be identified as author of this work has been asserted by him in accordance with sections 77 and 78 of the Copyright, Designs and Patents Act 1988.

All rights reserved. The purchase of this copyright material confers the right on the purchasing institution to photocopy or download pages which bear a copyright line at the bottom of the page. No other parts of this book may be reprinted or reproduced or utilised in any form or by any electronic, mechanical, or other means, now known or hereafter invented, including photocopying and recording, or in any information storage or retrieval system, without permission in writing from the publishers.

Trademark notice: Product or corporate names may be trademarks or registered trademarks, and are used only for identification and explanation without intent to infringe.

Library of Congress Cataloging-in-Publication Data
Names: Bailey, James A., 1963– author.
Title: Building learning capacity in an age of uncertainty: leading an agile and adaptive school / James A. Bailey.
Description: New York, NY: Routledge, 2021. |
Includes bibliographical references.
Identifiers: LCCN 2020052919 (print) | LCCN 2020052920 (ebook) |
ISBN 9780367701611 (hardback) | ISBN 9780367701604 (paperback) |
ISBN 9781003144847 (ebook)
Subjects: LCSH: School-based management. | Educational change. |
Educational leadership. | School improvement programs. |
School management and organization.
Classification: LCC LB2806.35 .B35 2021 (print) |
LCC LB2806.35 (ebook) | DDC 371.200973–dc23
LC record available at https://lccn.loc.gov/2020052919
LC ebook record available at https://lccn.loc.gov/2020052920

ISBN: 978-0-367-70161-1 (hbk)
ISBN: 978-0-367-70160-4 (pbk)
ISBN: 978-1-003-14484-7 (ebk)

Typeset in Optima
by Newgen Publishing UK

Access the Support Material:
www.routledge.com/9780367701604

This book is dedicated to my parents who gave me a love of reading and learning from an early age. As they always said, if somebody took the time to write a book, then it is worth the time and effort to consider it.

Contents

Acknowledgements   viii
Meet the Author   ix

1. Complexity, Agility, and Capacity   1
2. A New Model of Capacity for Learning   14
3. Capacity as Organizational Learning Processes   26
4. Capacity as Organizational Conditions   48
5. Capacity as Individual Skills and Beliefs   78
6. Capacity as Effective Teaming   105
7. Leading for Capacity Development   136
8. Back to the Future   156

Appendix A: Diagnostic for School Learning Capacity   172

Acknowledgements

I would like to acknowledge Heather Jarrow at the Routledge/Taylor Francis Group who has shepherded this book from its original idea to its finished form. She saw something in the idea and gave constant feedback to help make it a worthwhile addition to the field. I would also like to thank all my friends and colleagues over the years who waded through the ideas and drafts with me until they made sense. And as always, I want to thank my family who always indulge my reading and writing habits.

Meet the Author

James Bailey's career has encompassed teacher, principal, assistant superintendent, school turnaround leader, consultant, superintendent, and university teaching roles spanning Texas, Colorado, and Wyoming. As Superintendent in Wyoming, his district was the first member in the state to join the League of Innovative Schools after reform efforts around personalized learning and social-emotional development. In San Antonio, he led the turnaround efforts for the Carpe Diem Schools. His deep-seated commitment to equity and supporting school leaders led to his training as an executive coach and co-founding Brass Tacks Innovations focused on executive coaching of school and district leaders and helping them develop the capacity for sustained improvement and growth. He has a PhD in Educational Leadership and Innovation from the University of Colorado, is a prolific publisher and presenter, and currently serves as a core faculty member at Walden University in the area of educational leadership.

Complexity, Agility, and Capacity

As newly hired principal Amanda Lopez drove home, she felt a knot in her stomach from anxiety about her new position. Even though she had been a successful teacher in a neighboring town, being hired to reinvent Stonybrook High School had been quite a jump for her. As she turned to her day spent with her leadership team at a factory in town, she reflected on what she saw and what it meant for her school and students. Since the Covid-19 crisis in 2020, many schools had been struggling to find just the right model for educating their students, and pressure for high schools had increased with the demise of many institutions of higher education in the area.

In mid-summer, all of the administrative team in the Stonybrook district had been invited to go and see how the Stonybrook Food Company was using artificial intelligence in its factory. She had entered believing she would see lots of people working and a few machines. What she and her colleagues saw was something that would shake her beliefs about the new nature of work and what needed changing in her new school.

Inside the factory, which took potatoes and made them into frozen fries, tater tots and hash browns, she saw ten lines of potatoes being washed and cleaned, but not one human hand touched any of the potatoes. Only four humans were on the large floor, and they spent their entire time watching the screens in front of them and the robotic arms that removed the potatoes into various bins at the end of the line.

> When Amanda asked how many people were employed and what skills they needed, the factory manager told the administrative team that ten years ago there had been over 250 employed at this factor. Now they were down to 10 and had doubled their productivity due to the new automated process. As far as skills, he said, all of the line techs, as they were called, had at least a two-year degree in computer science and took screening tests for problem-solving skills, creativity, communication skills, and the ability to work as part of a team. The team also learned that no potato was touched by human hand until it reached the dinner table.
>
> As Amanda remembered what her day had been like, she wondered what it would take to help her staff recognize the new world their students faced.

There is no doubt that many of our schools today are remnants of a past era. Schools then were designed to solve specific problems and were organized around these problems, such as how do we group students, and how do we organize to be like the places our students will work? Schools also organized around what was to be taught—the curriculum—and ultimately around the primary purpose of schools at that time: the ability to separate students into various tracks. Many of these solutions still drive our mental models about schools today.

Schools in the past also developed during a specific historical context that remained relatively steady for an extended period. During the early parts of the twentieth century, our society, in general, was relatively static. No great industrial revolution occurred, therefore the organizational structure of schools could remain reasonably static. Cars emerged, as did radio and television, but none of these inventions significantly impacted how schools were designed or organized.

From the early 1990s until the early 2000's, however, society began to change with the advent of the digital revolution, the creation of semiconductors, personal computers, and the internet. New demands for higher cognitive skills emerged, and the standards-based era began attempting to make schools more aware of equity for all students. In one sense, this third iteration of the industrial revolution placed heavy demands on the capacity of schools and school systems to increase the learning of all students. Yet again, these drivers in our society did little to impact how schools were designed or organized.

Today, we have entered another significant time of disruption in our society. While previous authors have described this era as VUCA (volatile, uncertain, complex, and ambiguous) or the fourth industrial revolution, in March of 2020, a new era dawned upon American society, which has brought and will continue to bring significant changes to our communities. This era, labeled as the *Age of Uncertainty* in this book, was marked by a global pandemic, economic insecurity, increased racial inequities, and a marked polarization of our country.

These changes came at us with increased speed, scope, and impact (Schwab, 2016), which transformed all facets of our world, including education. Along with other societal drivers and demands, these changes have become interrelated and exponential in their growth. Because of this, schools over the next decade will need to develop newer forms of agile and adaptive learning capacity never before seen to meet these oncoming demands or risk becoming more obsolete.

The New Complex Contexts for Schools

> As Amanda Lopez drove to work the next morning her thoughts drifted back to her initial interview. Since most places were still in the post-pandemic lockdown, most of her interviews were done virtually. She did, however, get to meet the school interview team in person. Throughout that interview, she began to paint the picture in her mind of what had occurred at Stonybrook High School over the past few years. Over lunch she asked many questions and learned that the school's response had been less than coherent and many decisions about credits, schedules, and models still had not been fully worked out. While looking at the data, Ms Lopez also noticed that about 20% of students had still not been accounted for—mostly students of color and high poverty. As she pulled into the parking lot at Stonybrook High School, she wondered where those students had gone.

This book is both anticipatory and retrospective in nature. We know that new and exciting changes will be facing our society shortly, and the students we have in our care now will have to deal with the economic and learning challenges of these uncertain times. We also know that over the past two decades, we have learned a lot about how people, teams, and organizations can learn. However, we also know that schools often inherit the stress of society and will have to face and work within four complex contexts if they are to deliver on their promise to society.

Covid-19 Crisis

The Covid-19 crisis first appeared in the United States in March of 2020, and by mid-March, every brick-and-mortar school and school district had shuttered their doors and transitioned into some form of remote learning. Educators had to make a sudden shift into remote and online learning in various forms causing massive upheaval for them, their students, and their families.

Over time, as the pandemic impacted all facets of society, numerous cracks in the foundation of schooling as we knew emerged. Inequities exacerbated for students without broadband internet connections, and basic medical and nutritional needs were found to be lacking for many students. Diverse mental health needs of students who could not see their peers or teachers also emerged, and engagement for many students plummeted. All of these factors severely impacted learning, with some estimates showing that many students may have lost between a half and a full year of learning.

Because this worldwide pandemic will probably not be the last one seen, a new and different context has emerged for schools. New ideas of personalization for increased learning will need to be created, tried, and researched, along with the necessary skills for educators. New skills for students with self-direction and agency will also need further development, as will increased understanding of disease transmission and recovery. All these issues raise a unique set of challenges for schools.

Increased Focus on Equity

Simultaneously to the Covid-19 crisis, the death of George Floyd and other African-American citizen at the hands of police, caused massive protests in almost every state in the spring and summer of 2020. While equity has been a significant context for schools for many decades, the outpouring of grief, frustration, and protest across the US brought equity into the spotlight more than ever before. Some school districts canceled contracts with local police for school resource officers, and renewed efforts increased to disrupt systemic racism in American society, including public education.

With these efforts, a second important context was re-established for schools. Even with major civil rights movements starting with Brown v The Board of Education in 1954, by 2019 the segregation of US schools was still in place. The typical white student in the US attended a school that was 69% white while only making up 48% of the entire school population. Moreover, 40% of African-American and Latino attended highly segregated schools in which over 90% of students were students of color (Frankenberg, 2019).

Also, because of the Covid-19 crisis, many students did not have access to broadband internet limiting their opportunities to learn online, causing a widening of learning and achievement gaps. Because K-12 education is still the one universal institution in US society, new calls for increased focus on equity emerged.

Future Drivers

In addition to the recent events that create new contexts for schools, ongoing shifts in our society have and will continue to create new complex contexts for schools. Today, many authors and futurists (Schwab, 2016; Avenous, 2011), argue that we are entering the fourth industrial revolution. This fourth revolution, as do all revolutions, built off the previous ones and began at the turn of the twenty-first century. The fourth revolution can be classified as different than the digital revolution in that it:

- uses a much more mobile internet;
- includes more sensors and connected networks;
- utilizes artificial intelligence;
- enhances connectivity and relationships between things;
- impacts a broader scope of societal areas and will have an impact on jobs and the economy; and
- integrates numerous disciplines and discoveries.

According to Schwab (2016), the fourth industrial revolution leverages the inventions of the digital revolution and information technology age and is showing up in three primary areas of technology. The first is the physical world in which autonomous vehicles, 3D printing, advanced robotics, and new materials appear for use in numerous industries.

The second area is a continuation of the digital revolution but has now evolved into the internet of things. In this area of the fourth industrial revolution, the relationship is between the things and people through connected technologies and platforms. Think about the ability to attend meetings or even conferences online today, or the ability to set your thermostat from your car by phone. These digital platforms have decreased the friction for consumers, and many services now do not even have physical locations.

Last, the third area that helps us recognize a new era is in the biological field. Mapping the human genome and personalizing treatments for individuals is now in its early stages. Genetic engineering of foods and the use of bioprinting on 3D machines made for human skin and tissue will become more evident over time.

These technologies have already begun to impact education through the use of artificial intelligence in adaptive forms of software, more remote forms of professional learning, data interoperability, predictive learning analytics, virtual reality, big data, and learning algorithms. New curricula for these changes, along with an increased ethical responsibility that comes with the use of advanced technologies, all create a third and significant complex, context for schools.

Demands for New Organizational Forms and Leadership

The fourth complex context schools must contend with is the increasing demand for new organizational forms and ways of work and leadership. The need for new organizational structures and new forms of work is becoming more and more apparent. With high levels of employee disengagement and turnover (Corbin, 2017), people are searching for different ways to create a sense of purpose. "We know the way we are working is not working, but we cannot imagine an alternative. We long for change, but do not know how to get it" (Digman, 2019).

Organizational forms that still use command and control structures like schools are finding it more and more difficult to be fast and agile enough to meet the onslaught of increasing demands. Older organizational forms are beginning to buckle because of the stress thrust upon them. While most of the reform over the past two decades has focused on the curriculum, assessment, and instruction of teachers, few changes have managed to impact organizational forms and ways of work (Kim and Gonzales-Black, 2018). The hierarchical structures of most current school systems will no longer suffice, nor will the typical ways people are motivated and incentivized.

Laloux (2014) suggests that "every time humanity has shifted to a new stage, it has invented a new way to collaborate, a new organizational model." Organizations are the expression of our worldview about how things should work. Like us, they are in a current stage of redevelopment and, like humans, are stubbornly resistant to change. Laloux (2014), for instance, describes Amber organizations of which he includes public school systems as having highly formal roles in a hierarchy with top-down control and stability and conformity valued over all else.

In contrast, Green organizations may still have a hierarchy but focus highly on culture and empowerment to motivate employees. As a new context, schools will have to rethink many of their assumptions, which act like an operating system in the background to move to this type of organizational form. Assumptions around how to build teams, manage new initiatives, and develop employees for retention must be surfaced and rethought.

Adaptability and Agility: Meeting the Complex Future Head On

As she sat with her notebook of data and ideas, Amanda Lopez knew that the demands on her school were immense, but that the past ways of working to solve these problems would not suffice moving forward. In her past experience working in schools as a teacher, coach, and department chair, problems would usually be discussed for a short while until the next distractor emerged and the conversation would

> shift. It seemed to Ms. Lopez that the mental models of how problems and issues were solved in her staff would need to be shifted and that her school as an organization would need to be more nimble, agile, and adaptable to solve many of these issues.

Amid a new era for our society causing turbulence and uncertainty for schools, developing more adaptable and agile organizations that can respond to these needs will become increasingly important. This agility requires deeper learning capacity of individuals, teams, and organizations to meet the complexity of the future head on and productively help develop students for this era. The ability to learn deeply and integrate new learning into routines and behaviors exists as the only way that current schools will be able to meet the demands of this new era. In many industries, there has been a call to build on and extend these existing theories of organizational learning and to integrate concepts such as organizational learning, knowledge management, absorptive capacity, and learning capabilities (Vera et al. 2011).

In response, schools need to become more focused on organizing for learning versus organizing for execution. Organizing for execution refers to the assumptions that some thinkers make all the decisions and hand these down to the doers (Edmondson, 2019). In contrast, a true learning organization is one in which we treat the organizing principles more like a complex adaptive system. This type of organizing is more dynamic and adaptable due to a reliance on feedback around learning. This type of organization relies heavily on the learning of individuals and teams to help the organization information forage, intuit, interpret, integrate, and institutionalize new ideas demanded by the environment (Jenkin, 2013).

As new demands come from the external environment for schools and learning occurs, the ability to organize for learning emerges until a flywheel of learning about and from practice develops. Eventually, a new operating system appears that becomes more flexible and adaptable. Using the operating system analogy, if your current computer system is still running Windows 95, it cannot run today's modern software. It is outdated and lacks the sophistication for these newer programs. To meet the demands of these more complicated programs, you have to update your operating system to run faster with more memory to benefit from these more extensive, more complex programs. For today's schools the need exists to update our operating system toward more speed, adaptability, and memory. A new operating system for schools requires learning agility and adaptability, generative learning, and a new vision of the meaning of capacity.

Learning Agility and Adaptability

Over the past decade, as the environment has become increasingly volatile and fast-changing, numerous researchers have turned to knowledge-based concepts to help organizations understand how to manage this volatility. Organizational knowledge is a proven construct and provides a vital resource and source of competitive advantage (Vera et al., 2011). As one criterion for a new operating system for schools, learning agility defines as the fundamental speed of knowledge building and the belief that this new knowledge is useful and combines three interrelated concepts.

- *Absorptive capacity:* The basic definition of this concept is the ability to utilize externally held knowledge through (1) recognizing and understanding potentially valuable new knowledge outside the school; (2) assimilating valuable new knowledge; and (3) using the assimilated understanding to create new knowledge and outputs (Farrell et al., 2019). More specifically to education, some authors have used this concept to understand the degree to which schools and districts can best use guidance from external partners e.g. external knowledge. These authors suggest that the more absorptive capacity an organization has, the more it will benefit from engagement with new knowledge in the future. In short, absorptive capacity is the condition that allows a school to absorb and leverage external expertise.
- *Dynamic capability:* This concept bases on a similar idea that knowledge is a resource that can change over time (Della Corte and Del Gaudio, 2012). This concept centers significantly on the speed or dynamic of reconfiguring knowledge into new assets that a school can use. This concept also describes necessary knowledge-based activities such as knowledge acquisition, knowledge absorption, knowledge creation, knowledge storage, and knowledge combination and is highly linked to an organization's absorptive capacity (Della Corte and Del Gaudio, 2012).

- *Knowledge management:* Knowledge management is commonly used in knowledge-intensive organizations like schools to improve learning and development and solve one of the most significant problems in education. Individual teachers and teams create impactful knowledge frequently, yet there is typically no formal process to store and share this knowledge in most schools. "Knowledge management is a process of organizational practices involving sharing, storing, retrieving and transferring the knowledge possessed by individuals and groups in their daily operations, for pursuing long-term enhanced performance and development of organizations" (Cheng et al., 2017). In short, KM attempts to explain how knowledge is created, disseminated, and stored for ongoing use in organizations.
- *Knowledge building:* Often, schools will merely adapt what others are doing, which is known as adaptive learning or not rethinking mental models or paradigms. In contrast, more generative forms of learning and knowledge building are based on a school's specific context and "refers to a change in the mental model, paradigm, or knowledge through which we see reality" (Chiva, Grandino and Alegre, 2010). Knowledge building takes place in a well-defined problem space and produces knowledge which has a more public consideration to help build a common cognitive structure for the organization (Bereiter and Scardamalia, 2014). As schools continue to face more pronounced challenges, methods that contest old paradigms and build new knowledge will become an essential part of learning agility.

In sum, learning agility as a descriptor for a new operating system for schools is about the degree to which a school creates new knowledge, the speed at which it leverages that knowledge, and how that knowledge is managed for further use. New models and forms of capacity building for this type of ongoing learning will be needed to create this new operating system. We explore a new definition of capacity next.

A New Definition of Capacity

Since the early 1970's, the term capacity, organizational capacity, and capacity development have been used interchangeably and proposed as a significant resource that allows or enables change to occur (Berman and McLauglin, 1974). However, like many constructs used in education, the term capacity is used loosely and has been projected from many different theoretical perspectives. For instance, capacity has been defined as resources, structures, leadership, professional development, organizational conditions, and political capital.

If we genuinely want to understand capacity, we must have and use clear definitions from which a new framework can derive. This definitional clarity helps shape not only how we think and perceive ideas in the world but also supports the creation of a mental model that can be developed and refined through experiences. Spillane and Coldren (2011) captured the essence of this idea when they stated, "Hence, definitions are key analytical tools—working tools—and a very practical consideration when it comes to work on improving practice."

For this book, we propose the following definition and clarifications to help define capacity and takes into account learning agility plus what we know to date about capacity and organizational learning in all of its manifestations. The definition we are using for this book is:

Capacity as a noun means the set of defined processes and conditions that help a school organize for learning at the individual, team and organizational level around a central purpose. Over time this learning builds new knowledge and becomes a resource that can be drawn upon to improve agility and adaptability.

Capacity Development as a verb means using processes to promote interaction for learning at the individual, team, and organizational level to build more dynamic agility and adaptability.

From this base definition, we will explore a new model of capacity building in Chapter 2 that will help create a new operating system for schools in this age of uncertainty.

Team Considerations

1. Is your community and place of work facing this new era yet?
2. How would you describe the changes you are facing?
3. How are these new complex contexts in the age of uncertainty impacting you? Your school? How are you responding?

4. How is your school organized? For execution or learning?
5. How does your sense of capacity match the definition given?

References

Averous, J. (2011). *The fourth revolution: How to survive through the world's transformation.* Fourth Revolution Publishing.

Bereiter, C. and Scardamalia, M. (2014). Knowledge building and knowledge creation: One concept, two hills to climb. In S. C. Tan, H. J. So and J. Yeo (eds). *Knowledge creation in education* (35–52). Springer.

Berman, P. and McLauglin, M.W. (1974). *Federal programs supporting educational change: Vol 1, a model of educational change.* Rand Corporation. www.rand.org/pubs/reports/R1589z1.html

Cheng, E., Wu, S. and Hu, J. (2017). Knowledge management implementation in the school context; Case studies on knowledge leadership, storytelling, and taxonomy. *Educational Research for Policy and Practice,* 16 (2), 177–188; doi 10.1007/s10671-016-9200-0

Chiva, R., Grandio, A. and Alegre, J. (2010). Adaptive and generative learning: Implications from complexity theory. *International Journal of Management Reviews*; DOI: 10.1111/j.1468-2370.2008.00255.x

Corbin, J. (2017). *Surprising results from the 2017 Gallup employee engagement survey.* www.theemployeeapp.com/gallup-2017-employee-engagement-report-results-nothing-changed/

Della Corte, V. and Del Gaudio, G. (2012). Dynamic capabilities: A still unexplored issue with growing complexity. *Corporate Ownership & Control,* Vol 9 (4), 327–338.

Dignan, A. (2019). *Brave new work: Are you ready to reinvent your organization?* Portfolio/Penguin.

Edmondson, A. (2019). *The fearless organization: Creating psychological safety in the workplace for learning, innovation, and growth.* Wiley.

Farrell, C., Coburn, C. and Chong, S. (2019). Under what roles do school districts learn from external partrners? The role of absorptive capacity. *American Educational Research Journal,* 56 (3), 955–994. doi: 10.3102/0002831218808219

Frankenberg, E. (2019). What school segregation looks in the US today, in 4 charts. *The Conversation.* https://theconversation.com/what-school-segregation-looks-like-in-the-us-today-in-4-charts-120061

Jenkin, T.A. (2013). Extending the 4I organizational learning model: Information sources, forging processes and tools. *Administrative Sciences,* 3, 96–109; doi:10.3390/admsci3030096

Kim, A. and Gonzales-Black, A. (2018). *The new school rules. 6 vital practices for thriving and responsive schools.* Corwin Press.

Laloux, F. (2014). *Reinventing organizations: A guide to creating organizations inspired by the next stage of human consciousness.* Nelson Parker.

Schwab, K. (2016). The fourth industrial revolution: What it means and how to respond. www.weforum.org/agenda/2016/01/the-fourth-industrial-revolution-what-it-means-and-how-to-respond/

Spillane, J.P. and Coldren, A.F. (2011). *Diagnosis and design for school improvement: Using a distributed perspective to lead and manage change.* Teachers College Press.

Vera, D., Crossan, M. and Apaydin, M.A. (2011). A framework for integrating organizational learning, knowledge, capabilities, and absorptive Capacity. In Easterby-Smith, M. and Lyles, M. (eds), *Handbook of organizational learning and knowledge management,* (2nd edn, 153–180). Wiley.

A New Model of Capacity for Learning

> Amanda Lopez had heard a lot lately about the need for capacity and building capacity at her school from her district leaders especially since she had been asked to reform her school towards more personalized forms of learning after the Covid-19 crisis. Many suggested she needed a different vision, a different culture, more resources, more professional development, or more shared leadership to make this reform a reality. Many alluded to the idea that with better and more capacity in her school, student outcomes would improve. She had also read many similar ideas in articles and books in her graduate program as she prepared to become a principal. As she thought about all of the advice though, she could not remember any specific guidance or, for that matter, what capacity actually meant or how it exactly mattered. As she sat down to plan for her first year as principal, she began to ponder, she began to ponder what capacity meant precisely and how she could build it in her school.

In the previous chapter, we examined the new complex contexts in which schools are trying to adjust, and why a new vision for capacity as learning agility and its development is necessary. Since the early 1970s, many researchers have articulated the need for capacity (Berman and McLaughlin, 1977). Later work suggested that no matter how capacity and its development is defined, it needs to focus on enhancing the instructional core to promote more powerful instruction, especially to enhance equity. However, like many school leaders, Amanda Lopez needs a more fully formed set of ideas and routines for developing the necessary learning capacity in her school for success in the newer, complex contexts of today.

The purpose of this chapter is to review the conceptual foundations for a new model of learning capacity to help schools become more agile in meeting external demands. As a reminder, in Chapter 1, we defined capacity from this perspective as both a noun and a verb. The definition we are using for this book is:

Capacity as a noun means the set of defined processes and conditions that help a school organize for learning at the individual, team, and organizational level around a central purpose. Over time this learning builds new knowledge and becomes a resource that can be drawn upon to improve agility and adaptability.

Capacity Development as a verb means using processes to promote interaction for learning at the individual, team, and organizational level to build more dynamic agility and adaptability.

While not a complete literature review, this chapter gives the conceptual underpinning of the core concepts that went into the design of this new model of capacity for learning at multiple levels. Using these conceptual foundations, we introduce the model and briefly describe its systems and elements. Lastly, we will introduce leadership mindsets, skills, and routines as another form of capacity for developing agile learning capacity along with a description of the capacity diagnostic.

A New Model for Developing Learning Capacity

From her previous roles, Ms. Lopez knew that when a school focused on ongoing learning for everybody and this learning was shared and promoted, things changed more easily. She had also experienced that when school leaders were a part of this learning, people seemed to pay more attention to the importance of the ideas. While it seemed the most effective leaders led this learning with little effort, she knew she would need some sort of framework around which she could organize her school for learning.

A New Model of Capacity for Learning

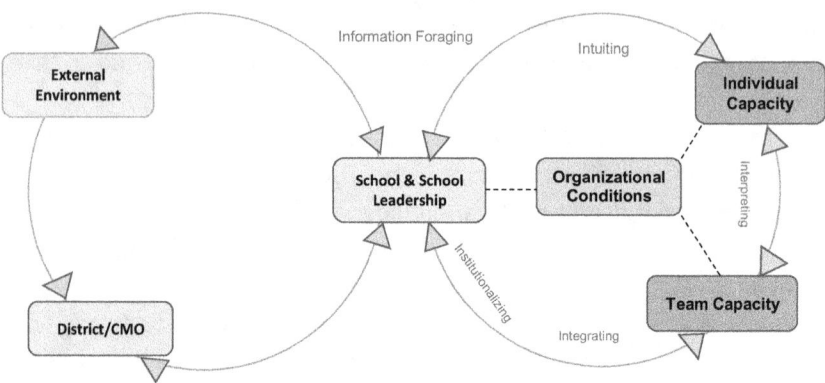

Figure 2.1 A New Model of Learning Capacity in Schools

When schools begin to organize for learning, the concepts from organizational, individual, and team learning can synthesize to create a new model for developing learning capacity for more agility (see Figure 2.1). I posit this model can create a new and different operating system that will allow schools to meet the challenges they face in this new era of uncertainty.

This new model for developing learning capacity is useful in that it helps us understand that learning at all levels is the primary function of all people in K-12 education. For this to happen, certain conditions, resources, systems, mindsets, and routines must be used to organize learning support.

There are very few models in the education field to date showing the interaction of individual, team, and organizational learning to support increasing agility.

The overall purpose of this new model, no matter the type or form of school, is to develop a school's capacity to:

1. Create learning agility to become more responsive to the complex contexts in which school now exist.
2. Continually learn about, improve and build knowledge around core instruction and learning through shared beliefs and mental models.
3. Continually learn about, innovate, and build knowledge around new demands from the environment.

4. Continually link individual, team and organization learning for improvement and innovation to build knowledge to improve student learning in all forms.
5. Continually develop individual and collective efficacy to take on more significant and critical problems.

However, what does a model of collective capacity for system reform look like in action? As Sharatt and Fullan (2009) suggested, "Capacity building is a highly complex, dynamic, knowledge-building process, is intended to lead to increased student achievement in every school ... And the key to driving this successful systemic capacity building ... is knowledge building that is universally aligned and coherent ...." In other words, "learning is the work" of capacity development. This new model helps to explain the generative and dynamic nature of this knowledge-building process.

In Figure 2.1, we can visualize the process. On the left side of the figure, the complex environment places new and difficult external demands on the district and school. The school and district help support one another around these environmental demands. For instance, the current demand for more personalized forms of learning influences both the school and district to begin an information-foraging process. Within the school organization, information foraging begins to drive the learning cycle when individuals or teams become more curious about some part of their practice in relation to the demand.

Processes of organizational capacity work to coherently support these demands and allow interaction at the individual learning level where people begin to intuit or discover and recognize patterns. As individuals begin to try these ideas and develop a sense of self-efficacy, they begin to work with teams to interpret the meaning of the demand. They ask how the demand fits their current mental model and beliefs about schools and learning, and what mental models and beliefs may have to be modified, deleted, or added to meet these demands. Over time, as these new mental models and beliefs begin to filter back to the organizational level through institutionalization processes, the systems and processes are engaged further. Knowledge building occurs and new knowledge is disseminated through networks in the school all supported by robust organizational conditions.

Note that the cycle on the right side does not just turn once but is ongoing. As soon as one person learns something new, the teams' mental model starts to shift and helps to modify the collective mental model of the organization. It is a "flywheel", as Collins (2019) discusses. It turns slowly at first, but over time gains momentum, developing strategic compounding in which each step is "an inevitable consequence of the step before it" (Collins, 2019). So what enables this flywheel or learning cycle to gain this momentum? Let's examine the foundations of each layer of learning that make up this new capacity building model.

Capacity as Organizational Processes for Learning

If capacity is ultimately about the capability of individuals, teams, and the organization to learn, then the concepts underlying organizational learning need more precision as many previous descriptions of this concept have led to confusion. To simplify things, this new model primarily uses Jenkins' 5i model (Jenkins, 2013), giving us a more process-oriented way to show how the external environment can influeence organizational learning. This model shows organizational learning as a five-step process which encompasses multiple levels—individual, groups, and organization—and includes feedback as a systemic element. These processes include:

1. Information foraging defined as the intentional process or mechanism to search and scan the environment to trigger the intuiting stage.
2. Intuiting defined as the process to recognize patterns and insights for interesting possibilities.
3. Interpreting is defined as the process to develop shared understanding at the individual and team levels and updating of mental models.
4. Integrating defined as the process to take the shared mental models and translate them into a coordinated action.

5. Institutionalizing defined as the process to embed the action into organizational routines, procedures, and "cultural code" (Jenkins, 2013).

This level also includes specific processes for improvement and innovation. These are the actual processes used to create and generate knowledge and differentiate between improving what currently happens (reading instruction, for instance) versus using more agile or innovation processes to add new curricula or instructional methods (personalized learning, for instance). These processes will be discussed more in Chapter 3.

Capacity as Organizational Conditions for Learning

Cabrera and Cabrera (2015) define any organization as a system of systems that can arrange or develop to help solve the "wicked problems". From the research base, this new model of capacity building utilizes essential conditions that help support the development of capacity for learning at the organizational level. These organizational conditions will be explored more thoroughly in Chapter 4.

These conditions include:

1. Systems for *clarity of purpose and instructional guidance* that help create shared mental models and beliefs
2. Systems for *creating coherence* that help connect and align all of these pieces for improving teaching and learning.
3. Systems for *distributing leadership* that help create shared ownership and leadership for school decisions and processes, especially as they pertain to supporting learning.
4. Systems for *creating positivity* that help generate meaning, purpose, and virtue among staff. This system is the critical fuel for the ongoing work of learning that needs to occur and includes a school's shared beliefs around equity and the cultural capital of students.
5. Systems for *knowledge management* that help codify, store, and use newly built knowledge.

Capacity as Individual Skills and Beliefs for Learning

From the capacity literature and latest findings from cognitive science, this new model looks at five concepts that focus on ways to support and develop individual beliefs and learning. Supported by specific organizational conditions and processes, adult learning and development can grow and help support team and organizational learning through shared mental models and beliefs (Rook, 2013). These concepts will be explored more thoroughly in Chapter 5.

1. *Expertise* will help us understand how leaders need to take into account the developmental stages of teachers and what it takes to develop expertise.
2. Habit development and *deliberate practice* will help leaders see why deliberate practice is necessary to develop new skills beyond just receiving feedback
3. *Belief systems* and mental models will help leaders understand how they form and how to modify them toward a more shared understanding.
4. *Self-efficacy* will help leaders know if and when teachers are developing efficacy in their craft and how to help teachers develop this belief system.
5. *Conceptual change* using the CAMCC model will show leaders how teachers can potentially change their conceptual models and embrace new ideas.

Capacity as Effective Teaming for Learning

From the capacity and team and team learning literature, this new model looks at four concepts that focus on how the capacity for team learning emerges so that individuals can share and modify their mental models and beliefs. These will be explored more thoroughly in Chapter 6.

1. Elements of *teaming* will help leaders see why teaming is an active learning strategy and how to help teams develop effective teaming strategies.

2. How and if *team learning* is occurring will help leaders understand the essential focus for teams and the support of individuals.
3. The role of *psychological safety* will help leaders and teams understand the crucial element of teaming and how it develops.
4. *Collective efficacy* will help leaders understand another important outcome from teaming and how to help teams develop this collective belief system.

Capacity as Leadership for Learning

This book is not about leadership per se, but about how leaders in a collective and distributed fashion work to develop the capacity for more organizational, individual, and team learning. Rather than focus on the individual perspective of leadership, we take a more distributed perspective and look at mindsets, skills, and the actual routines formal or informal leaders need to use to develop learning capacity.

The nature of leadership in this model shows that to help develop a more agile form of learning capacity, all leaders must develop certain mindsets that will engage the development of skills through the use of specific routines (see **Figure 2.2**). This framing helps move the concepts of leadership from theory to practice.

Why focus on leadership mindsets, skills, and routines within this model?

First, as discussed in Chapter 1, new complex contexts will require educational leaders to learn how to develop more agile learning organizations to adapt to this new environment. These changing contexts will require leaders to develop new mental models and paradigms about their roles. These new ways of thinking about roles require different mindsets or beliefs around capacity as learning.

Second, a routine defines as a "repetitive, recognizable pattern of interdependent actions involving multiple actors" (Feldman, 2003). An organizational routine in simpler terms is repeatable, recognizable, and involves two or more staff members, not just the official leader (Feldman, 2003). The daily meeting of a grade-level team is a routine, as is what they focus on and accomplish during these meetings. New routines will be needed to create a new operating system for a school that wants to develop an enhanced capacity for more significant or

A New Model of Capacity for Learning

Capacity Model Area	Leadership Mindsets
Capacity as Organizational Conditions	• Creating the right conditions for growth • Distributing leadership • Creating positivity
Capacity as Organizational Processes	
1. Information foraging	• Future oriented • External orientation
2. Intuiting (individual learning)	• Recognizing insights • Sense making
3. Interpreting (individual and team learning)	• Crafting meaning
4. Integrating (individual and team learning)	• Creating feedback loops for adaptability • Connecting people and teams
5. Institutionalizing (organizational learning)	• Crafting coherence and accountability
Cross cutting mindsets	• Generating learning • Building knowledge • Curiosity • Communicating and connecting

Figure 2.2 Leadership Mindsets for Building Learning Capacity

more sophisticated forms of learning. These new routines are similar to the new sections in updated software that allow you to perform more complicated actions.

Finally, routines have also been considered a significant part of organizational learning (Feldman, 2003). Routines can help leaders and teams with information foraging, intuiting, interpreting, and integrating; they become embedded as an institutionalized feature of a school using the 5I framework for organizational learning introduced above. In essence, they assist in learning at all three levels. Routines frequently become part of the schema of organizations when used. Over time they become institutionalized to help with stability, and new ones can be attempted and modified to help with change efforts.

In each of the following, Chapters 3–6, we will explore these leadership mindsets, skills, and routines leaders can use along with a brief explanation of the learning system for each layer of capacity.

Diagnosing Your School's Capacity

> As Ms. Lopez began to make sense this model of capacity building, she also pondered how she would know the level of capacity her school possessed so she could determine areas of need. Just like when she went to the doctor for her annual physical, she needed a diagnostic tool to help her figure out the learning health of her school.

This chapter discussed how with the right conditions, systems, mindsets, and routines in place, capacity for learning will be developed at the individual, team, and organizational levels. As a new "operating system," this model can help schools develop an ongoing flywheel for enhanced learning agility. In a sense, it creates a pedagogy for the school as a system organized for learning at the individual, team, and organizational levels. As the McKinsey (2010) report stated: "for a system's improvement journey to be sustained over the long term, the improvements have to be integrated into the very fabric of the system pedagogy." To see how impactful your school's learning systems are currently, a diagnostic tool will allow your school to determine areas of strength and opportunities for growth that can be used to gauge progress. See Appendix A for the complete tool. You can use the complete diagnostic, or focus on sections associated with each chapter, as these will also be discussed in the corresponding chapters.

Team Considerations

1. How would you define capacity for learning? How do you know your school has it or not?
2. Which steps in the 5i process are familiar to you? What similar steps do you take in your school's learning or improvement cycles?
3. How do you differentiate between improvement and innovation?
4. Why are beliefs and self-efficacy so hard to change and develop in people?

5. Why is teaming such a vital system to create in a school? Why is psychological safety so challenging to create on school teams? Why is collective efficacy so important?
6. What types and forms of capacity have you tried to develop? What routines do you have in place now to help with the learning for adults? How have they helped?
7. How are things learned by teams or individuals stored and disseminated in your school?
8. Are the adults in your organization naturally learning and developing on a day to day basis? Is this possible?
9. What kinds of routines do you personally employ to develop the learning of adults in your school?
10. Is the learning flywheel spinning in your organization, or are there lots of starts and stops?

References

Berman, P. and McLaughlin, M. (1977). *Federal programs supporting educational change Vol VII: Factors affecting implementation and continuation.* RAND Corporation.

Cabrera, D. and Cabrera, L. (2015). *Systems thinking made simple: New Hope for solving wicked problems.* Pletica Publishers: Kindle edition.

Collins, J. (2019). *Turning the flywheel.* HarperCollins Publishers. Kindle edition.

Feldman, M. S. and Pentland, B. T. (2003). Reconceptualizing organizational routines as a source of flexibility and change. *Administrative Science Quarterly*, 48, 94–118.

Jenkins, T.A. (2013). Extending the 4I organizational learning model: Information sources, foraging processes and tools. *Administrative Sciences*, 3, 96–109; doi:10.3390/admsci3030096

King, M.B. and Bouchard, K. (2011). The capacity to build organizational capacity in schools. *Journal of Educational Administration*, 49 (6), 653–669, doi.org/10.1108/09578231111174802

McKinsey (2010). *How the world's most improved school systems keep getting better.* McKinsey & Company, www.mckinsey.com/industries/public-and-social-sector/our-insights/how-the-worlds-most-improved-school-systems-keep-getting-better

Rook, L. (2013). Mental models: A robust definition. *Learning Organization,* 20 (1), 38–47.

Sharrat, L. and Fullan, M. (2009). *Realization: The change imperative for deepening district-wide reform.* Corwin Press.

Capacity as Organizational Learning Processes

> In her principal preparation program at a local university, Amanda Lopez had been asked to read about organizational learning. At first, she had a hard time grasping how organizations could learn. As she dug deeper into the concept, however, she began to understand that the patterns and taken-for-granted processes in a school were a form of learning. These processes, like a bell schedule, had become part of the daily habits and routines of a school.
>
> As she took stock of her first month on the job, she could easily see processes in place for issues such as taking care of attendance and tardies and deciding student eligibility. What she could not see, however, were the routines for creating new knowledge and spreading new ideas between departments and individuals even though she saw how many of her teachers were working hard to develop student learning solutions.
>
> When she asked about how ideas were shared and disseminated across the building at her department chair meetings, she was met with a long silence and averted eye glances. Finally, the science department chair said, "I didn't know we were supposed to? Isn't that one more thing we would have to find time for?"
>
> As Ms. Lopez closed the meeting that day, she wondered what precisely organizational learning meant at a large school like hers, and what she had to do to make this a reality among all the other things that needed to be improved.

When Peter Senge's (1990) seminal work on the learning organization was first published, many educators quickly latched onto the ideas around mental models, personal mastery, and team learning. What many struggled with were the concepts of systems thinking and organizational learning. Like Amanda Lopez, many school and system leaders could not understand what organizational learning meant, where the brain was in an organization, and the processes for storing new knowledge. Like many ideas in education, without a clear framework and set of steps to use, powerful ideas like organizational learning are put on the back burner.

To use a concept like organizational learning, leaders must first possess a deep understanding of the concept then be able to translate it into concrete steps for their teachers. The problem is that many of the assumptions around the concept of organizational learning were never clarified for leaders. Many authors use the term "organizational learning", loosely assuming leaders know what it means and how it works. Organizational learning, like many other concepts, has become a taken-for-granted notion.

For this new model to be effective, school leaders need to understand organizational learning as a form of capacity that helps build new knowledge. They also need an elementary explanation of critical ideas with a set of steps to employ it. We start with some basic ideas to gain some clarity around this form of learning for capacity development. For our purposes, the concept of organizational learning uses these interrelated ideas:

1. First, organizational learning has to *balance the new and the old*. Many older processes and routines still work well. They have become institutionalized. Somebody, many years ago, created a process to handle some problem, which now is a given. Organizational learning in this new model, though, is about strategic renewal which improves processes that may not be working or adding entirely new ones for different purposes and needs.

2. Second, organizational learning is also about *knowledge building* around core problems of practice. Because solutions have to function within the local context, most problems at their core have to be solved locally through knowledge building. At a fundamental level, knowledge is created by individuals and teams. Organizational learning includes processes that amplify the knowledge created by individuals and teams (Ortenbland, 2018).

3. Third, organizational learning is about *how the different levels integrate* and spread new knowledge. Because schools often only focus on the individual learning of teachers, the implementation and spread of new ideas is often stunted. Studies in other fields find that organizations engaging in learning practices at one level are more likely to engage in practices at another level. "While organizational learning is more than the sum of ILP (individual learning processes) and TLP (team learning processes), they make possible organizational learning" (Krylova, Vera and Crossan, 2016).

4. Fourth, organizational learning focuses on the *process of learning* versus the content of that learning. Much implementation and change in education addresses the content of the change, whether it be a new curriculum, teaching technique, or operational procedure. The point here is that most change in education treats new knowledge as facts to be learned, then wonders why behavior does not change. Organizational learning treats learning as how learning happens and diffuses it.

5. Finally, "… organizational learning is the process of change in individual and shared thought and action, which is affected by and *embedded in the institutions* of the organization" (Vera et al., 2011). Therefore, we can say that, "When individual and group learning becomes institutionalized, organizational learning occurs and knowledge is embedded in non-human repositories such as routines, systems, structures, culture, and strategy" (Crossan et al.,1999).

Organizational learning as a primary learning level in this new model continually builds new knowledge which accumulates in individuals, teams, and school routines. Organizational learning evolves into the core, comprehensive process a school uses for implementation and strategic renewal. It is the process through which all other levels of learning interact to create capacity for learning, which again defines as:

Capacity as a noun means the set of defined processes, and conditions that help a school organize for learning at the individual, team, and organizational level around a central purpose. Over time this learning builds new knowledge and becomes a resource that can be drawn upon to improve agility and adaptability.

Capacity Development as a verb means using processes to promote interaction for learning at the student, staff, team, and organizational level to build more dynamic agility and adaptability.

This chapter will examine the organizational learning system more in-depth using a specific process model, discuss unique learning processes, examine ways to diagnose this system in schools, and explain routines leaders can use to develop this comprehensive learning system.

The 5i Organizational Learning Process

> During a meeting of her leadership meeting, Ms. Lopez had asked the question about what team members thought about their current implementation and learning processes. What she heard did not surprise her. Comments like "too rushed, not enough time to figure things out, too many new things, and no feedback loops to know if changes were having an impact" were forthcoming. One teacher summarized it well when he said, "It seems like we are too linear. We don't learn in cycles like we try to do in our classrooms. We need to think more in learning cycles." Ms. Lopez smiled when she heard this comment. It fit right into what she had been thinking about all Fall.

To help Ms. Lopez and her team better understand organizational learning, this capacity building model utilizes Jenkins' 5i model (Jenkins, 2013). The 5i model takes into account the role of searching and responding to the external environment, which is vital for handling complexity in our world today. It is one of the few researched models that accounts for the interaction of individual, team and organizational learning similar to the model proposed in this book (see **Figure 3.1**).

The 5i model proposes that learning is a highly dynamic process that includes feed-forward and feedback processes, noted by the two-way arrows in the figure. These processes span the individual, group, and organizational levels and include information foraging, intuiting, interpreting, integrating, and institutionalizing. These processes are the major stages that bind learning capacity together for a school. Each of these is examined below accompanied by a small vignette to help exemplify each stage.

Organizational Learning Processes

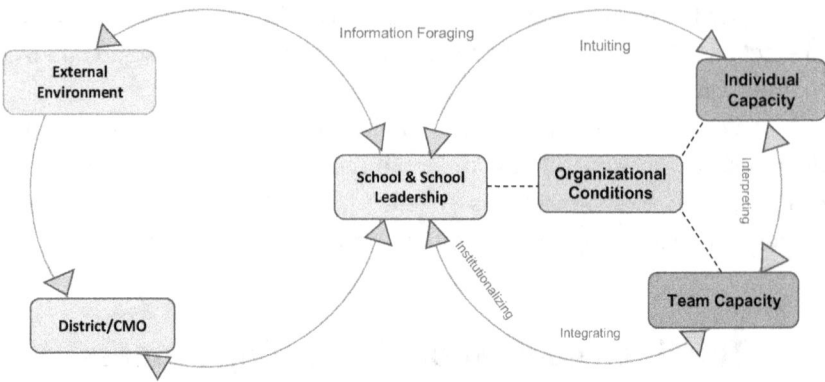

Figure 3.1 Organizational Learning Processes as Capacity

Information Foraging

> As a first move to become more of a learning organization, Amanda Lopez created a future-oriented task force whose primary role was to gather information on new trends in education and broader trends in society overall that might impact Stonybrook High School. Since nobody on staff had this background, the task force hired an external consultant to offer a series of workshops and related resources to help gather this type of information. Members of the task force were also charged to lead and share this information with smaller teams in the school.

This stage is an evolutionary process that involves scanning the external environment through recognizing, searching, or experiencing new ideas and knowledge. It describes the process by which information sources and search spaces are chosen, navigated, and assessed (Jenkins, 2013).

Intuiting

> As the future-oriented task force was learning with their consultant, individually, they were being asked to come up with various metaphors

Organizational Learning Processes

> and visuals to understand what was happening in the external environment for their school. They also met with Ms. Lopez and had many discussions to develop common metaphors and visuals to try on with their teams. During meetings with their smaller teams, each team leader used these metaphors and visuals to introduce future ideas and potential needs for their students.

This stage of the organizational learning process is typically done at the individual learning level and involves recognizing patterns and insights into new ideas. Experiences, visuals, and metaphors are essential inputs to use during this stage to build common mental models.

Interpreting

> As their time with the consultant ended, the task force continued to meet and make sense of all they had learned. Their discussions created a shared mental model among the team members of what the world of work would demand from their students. After lengthy discussions with the smaller teams, the task force decided that the area of social-emotional learning was an area to pursue as they saw that this form of learning helped create more well-rounded people.
>
> Now that there was a prevailing direction, the task force decided that the intuiting and interpreting stages needed various learning methods. This group created various book studies, found online courses, and integrated design labs into their meetings. Department PLC's (Professional Learning Communities) were also used to help understand and create the connections between academic content and social–emotional learning.

This stage of the learning process usually begins with individual learning but moves to a team learning process. Interpreting involves developing collective meaning and understanding and creating shared mental models among the team members. During this stage, new ideas are formed, discussed, debated, and common mental models formed among the team. This stage has a tight connection with the integration stage in that much of the interpretation of an idea comes about by actually using the idea, making adjustments, reinterpreting it, and trying again. Well facilitated dialogue and discussions are typical inputs used in this stage.

Integrating

> At this stage, there had been lots of learning by teachers at Stonybrook High but little movement of these ideas into practice. Small teams designed ways that social–emotional learning could be moved into practice using the task force members as leaders. The school's advisory period was designated as the primary space for this form of learning, but other techniques and models were chosen to be used during regular class time.
>
> During this stage, the smaller teams also moved back and forth between their trials in the integration stage and interpretation stage. Teams examined the impact on students, and the shared mental models were surfaced, adjusted, and deepened through reflection. This process exemplifies the real idea of feedback in that teams tried something, collected data on its impact, and used that data to make sense of it and adjust for their next trials. This process also exemplifies the core of knowledge building. Teams and individuals took what they knew at the time, tried it, and used the results to build new and more profound knowledge about their initiative.

This stage of the organizational learning process occurs at the team level, where the shared mental models and understanding of the new idea translates into action. This stage integrates tightly with the interpreting stage in that application and revision of the process helps deepen the interpretation and understanding of the idea. Dialogue, discussion, and design processes are useful in this stage.

Institutionalizing

> At this stage, the learning at Stonybrook High School had started to become institutionalized, although there was always more to learn. Teaching SEL had become a standard routine embedded within their advisory program, and PLC's had been formed to continue exploring new ideas and the impact of their SEL program on student growth.

This final stage occurs at the organizational level when the learning that has happened through the previous stages becomes embedded into routines and procedures and is part of the organizational culture. In this stage, knowledge management systems and routines increase.

In brief, note that organizational learning in this new capacity-building model is not just a planning routine. This more extensive learning process opens the school up to the external demands of society and helps build new knowledge through other learning processes that eventually become institutionalized over time. Also, note that outside experts can and will be used in the early stages of intuiting and interpretation.

In contrast, most implementation processes stop at the intuiting level, leaving it up to individuals to make their interpretation and figure out integration on their own. In our estimation, this is why many great ideas have never become institutionalized. Most of these new ideas require social learning to figure out how to integrate them into daily practice. While the individual learning of teachers is paramount, the role of the team and organization needs to be highly supportive in supporting individual learning and building of new beliefs.

Special Learning Processes

There are other special organizational learning processes that are quite similar to the 5i process. These relate to the lean startup ideas that have revolutionized the business world (Ismail et al., 2014). Since most organizations, including schools, are not set up to withstand risk and change and often reject changes outright, "constant experimentation and process iteration are now the only ways to reduce risk" (Ismail et al., 2014). According to Ismail et al. (2014), "Large number of bottom-up ideas, properly filtered, always trump top-down thinking no matter the industry or organization." Two such methods are explored below.

Improvement Science Processes

Building collective knowledge is a challenging but necessary process if schools are going to handle the complexity of our times. Improvement science is a specific form of organizational learning but fits within the general 5i processes.

Improvement science started in industry then the health care field but found its way to education through the Carnegie Foundation for the Advancement of Teaching. Its origins in education resulted from a frustration with current methods of implementation in which little follow-up or iteration happened around some excellent reform ideas. According to Bryk et al. (2015), "So a good idea found itself embedded in a bad development strategy with weak collective will, limited capacity to execute, and an unrealistic timetable."

Further, in most of the reform efforts, there was no intentional system to capture, transform, and refine knowledge gained to help accelerate implementation. Much research has suggested that these reform efforts resulted in "going fast and learning slow" when, in fact, complex problems in education require "learning fast to implement well" (Bryk et al., 2015).

Improvement Science focuses on the specific work or tasks people do and uses rapid tests of change to "guide the development, revision, and continued fine-tuning of new tools, processes, work roles, and relationships. This approach is explicitly designed to accelerate learning by doing" (Bryk et al., 2015). The goal in improvement research is not to try and pilot something, but to create knowledge around a reform idea to help it spread faster and with more significant impact. Improvement science is a learning-focused methodology which uses disciplined inquiry to improve practice.

Improvement science always centers on finding evidence and utilizing three highly specific questions:

- What is the specific problem I am trying to solve?
- What change might I introduce and why?
- How will I know whether the change is actually an improvement?

To help focus on the creation of new knowledge through disciplined inquiry methods, Improvement Science utilizes six principles that help knowledge building and learning happen.

- *Make the work problem-specific and user-centered:* This is a key to learning—having a very well-agreed upon and specific problem to solve.
- *Focus on variation in performance:* Variability is a normal state for most schools and focuses on "what works, for whom, and under what conditions."
- *See the system that produces the current outcomes:* This principle fits well into the new model of capacity building in that we need to understand all of the elements that may be causing the problem and using all levels of learning to solve it.
- *We cannot improve at scale what we cannot measure:* Practical measurement of specific processes and other outcomes are critical for timely and specific feedback loops.
- *Use disciplined inquiry to drive improvement:* Using small, timely experiments that allows adaptive integration of new ideas and techniques into the local context. This principle fits well into the 5i process of interpreting and integrating.
- *Accelerate learning through networked communities:* This principle lies at the heart of organizational learning in that it takes the individual, team, and the whole school to become networked to create new knowledge from learning (Bryk et al., 2015).

Improvement Science is a specific and disciplined way of knowledge creation and learning which matches well to the 5i model of organizational learning. The primary aim of Improvement Science is to improve a school's ability to improve over time by building learning capacity about proposed changes.

Design Thinking

Similarly, design thinking counters the call for researched-based solutions prevalent in our schools today, since many demands from the external environment do not, as yet, have clear researched-based solutions. Many of these changes can be labeled as adaptive changes since we have to learn our way through them which requires knowledge building (Heifitz, 1999).

Rather than moving from a predisposed solution in search of a problem, design thinking is another structured learning process. This process uses the wisdom of the local educators to generate and develop solutions to their most pressing issues. Schools and classrooms face design challenges all the time that range on a continuum from simple to complex and which often demand a disciplined approach. For instance, deciding on a room arrangement for seating is a design challenge as is figuring out how to engage students around difficult content or recreating a whole school experience for students. No matter the degree of complexity of the challenge, design thinking engages educators around a systematic process to see what works in their local context.

Design Thinking is also similar to other lean methods in its reliance on quick experimentation to come up with ideas, try them out, gather feedback, and iterate again and again. For instance, think about trying to teach students the process of having a good discussion. Typically, this technique turns into an argument with more emotion than reasoning. However, imagine that a team of teachers designs new techniques, tries them out, and continually iterates these ideas until this technique becomes second nature to teachers and students.

Design Thinking also uses predetermined phases similar to the 5i processes to help design solutions to specific problems and include (Design Thinking for Educators):

- *Discovery:* In this step, a specific design challenge is defined. This challenge needs to be framed using a "How might we ..." question with a big enough challenge to matter.

- *Interpretation:* Once stories, conversations, data, and field notes are gathered, the next phase is to take all of this information and make some sense of it. During this phase, people share their learning and insights from the stories they heard. From this information, teachers connect the various strands of insight into themes and create visual reminders.
- *Ideation:* Once the problem is better understood through the interpretation stage, the ideation phase focuses on generating lots of ideas to answer the "How might we ..." question. Ideation happens through brainstorming, drawing, or other techniques and should generate lots of ideas if done well.
- *Experimentation:* Once an idea has evolved to this phase, prototypes can be created to use. Prototypes can take the form of diagrams, stories, models, or role-plays. Once, a prototype is built, it can be used or tried in a live situation to gather feedback on how well it might work. During this phase, teams also have to determine the type of feedback to gather and how to gather it.
- *Evolution:* In the final phase of design thinking, the design concept develops more fully over time. During this phase, teams plan next steps and document progress as the design idea gets used in more real-life contexts and begins to impact the intended users. During this phase, teams also begin to measure the indicators of success to see how the idea is impacting users.

Design Thinking is another lean method that is learning focused, and matches the processes of the 5i model of organizational learning. The primary aim of Design Thinking is to use the creativity of a school's staff to develop more contextual solutions to pressing problems and learn from the ongoing process.

In sum, "Knowledge gives you a little bit of an edge, but tinkering (trial and error) is the equivalent of 1,000 IQ points. It is tinkering that allowed the Industrial Revolution" (Taleb, 2012). To meet the complexity of the era of uncertainty organizational learning forms that allow for speedy iteration help develop a school's agility

Diagnosing this Level of Capacity Building

Developing organizational learning capacity in a school is a considerable skill that most school leaders have not learned. Learning at this level requires a systemic perspective about how all processes and forms of learning can and should relate to one of the major processes of the 5i model. As the father of the lean-startup movement states, "The modern rule of competition is whoever learns fastest, wins" (Ries, 2011). We would modify this sentiment and suggest that the modern rule of dealing with complexity for schools is whoever learns fastest, wins for their students.

To get a general sense on how well your school uses organizational learning processes, take a few minutes and take this part of the school diagnostic (see **Figure 3.2**) individually or as a team.

Leading to Develop Organizational Learning Processes

Leading for organizational learning will require a different set of mindsets and skills that can lead to learning. Again, when we discuss leaders and leadership this includes not only formal leaders but also informal leaders in a distributed manner. Below, we list out these mindsets and skills that leaders need to develop organizational learning processes (see **Figure 3.3**). These mindsets and skills will be examined further in the next few chapters.

Routines for Organizational Learning Processes

Organizational learning has five major processes in which all other forms of learning happen. Leaders need specific routines in each stage to help foster learning within these stages. The routines briefly described below can help foster organizational learning capacity in each stage. The specific routines for each stage of the organizational learning process are briefly described below show how leaders and leadership teams can foster organizational learning capacity in each stage (see **Figure 3.4**).

Organizational Learning Processes

Organizational Learning Processes: The school develops and uses organizational processes to support ongoing learning about external demands and areas for internal improvement.

Processes at this level of learning	Diagnostic Questions	Responses 1. Highly inaccurate 2. Somewhat in accurate 3. Not sure 4. Somewhat accurate 5. Highly accurate				
1. 5i organizational learning process	1a. Our school has a method to scan the external environment for ideas that will help our school	1	2	3	4	5
	1b. When considering new ideas, our school allows us time to generate insights and patterns	1	2	3	4	5
	1c. When considering new ideas, we create shared mental models together	1	2	3	4	5
	1d. When considering new ideas our team/school develops coordinated actions to try them out	1	2	3	4	5
	1e. When considering new ideas our team/school uses cycles to refine the idea	1	2	3	4	5
	1f. Many of the new ideas we have considered become common routines or processes in our school.	1	2	3	4	5
	1g. When trying new ideas, we often generate new knowledge about the idea.	1	2	3	4	5
		Total ____/7 =				

Figure 3.2 Organizational Learning Processes Diagnostic

Organizational Learning Processes

Processes at this level of learning	Diagnostic Questions	Responses
2. Special learning processes	2a. Our school often uses cycles of inquiry to generate new learnings about a problem of learning	1 2 3 4 5
	2b. Our school uses different learning methods for new innovative ideas versus improving what we already do.	1 2 3 4 5
	2c. We often iterate on ideas to make them work for our students	1 2 3 4 5
	2d. In our learning processes we often collect various forms of data	1 2 3 4 5
	2e. We often consider the needs of our students when designing new trials	1 2 3 4 5
	2f. We often generate new insights during our cycles of learning	1 2 3 4 5
	2g. We often use a common design process to solve common problems of practice.	1 2 3 4 5 Total ____/7=

Figure 3.2 (Cont.)

Organizational Learning Process	Leadership Mindsets	Leadership Skill(s)
1. Information foraging	• Future oriented • External orientation	1. Scanning the environment 2. Initiating and cultivating engagement 3. Seeing connections among systems 4. Jointly determining problems and needs 5. Developing team processing

Figure 3.3 Leadership Mindsets and Skills for Organizational Learning Processes

Organizational Learning Process	Leadership Mindsets	Leadership Skill(s)
2. Intuiting (individual learning)	• Recognizing insights • Sense making	1. Working with beliefs and clarifying mental models 2. Leading systematic processing 3. Influencing efficacy 4. Noticing hidden patterns
3. Interpreting (individual and team learning)	• Crafting meaning	1. Developing and analyzing teaming and using learning processes 2. Creating psychological safety 3. Influencing collective efficacy 4. Building short inquiry cycles and narrowing to action 5. Developing team processing
4. Integrating (individual and team learning)	• Creating feedback loops for adaptability • Connecting people and teams	1. Helping others design and build ideas and running inquiry cycles 2. Fostering disciplined inquiry and understanding impact 3. Helping others learn from their actions/reinforcing 4. Reframing connections and integrating ideas 5. Helping others stay open
5. Institutionalizing (organizational learning)	• Crafting coherence and accountability	1. Building precise language and a common knowledge base 2. Sustaining focus 3. Amplifying success and deviance and moving toward precision 5. Unifying

Figure 3.3 (Cont.)

Organizational Learning Processes

Organizational Learning Process	Leadership Mindsets	Leadership Skill(s)
Cross cutting themes	• Generating learning • Building knowledge • Curiosity • Communicating and connecting	1. Communicating explicitly and challenging the status quo 2. Building curiosity in others and developing clear theories of action 3. Developing team processes 4. Building relationships and trust 5. Connecting people and creating networks 6. Learning alongside and building personal knowledge 7. Seeing the system, the details and their interconnections

Figure 3.3 (Cont.)

Routine Name: Information Foraging/ External Scanning	**Routine Name: Intuiting Routine**
Uses: This routine can be used to help know and anticipate trends that may impact or influence your school in the future.	*Uses*: This routine can be used at the individual and team level to discern patterns and concepts from proposed change ideas. This routine uses visuals, metaphors and analogies to help discern these patterns and concepts.

Process Steps:
1. Create a team whose sole purpose is to scan the environment.
2. Create a knowledge management system like a shared Google drive with various folders.
	Process Steps:
	1. Teachers learn about a specific change idea.
	2. Have teachers either
	  (a) Draw a picture of what the change looks like to them, or
	  (b) Have them write a metaphor: this idea is like _____ because.

Figure 3.4 Routines for Organizational Learning Processes

Organizational Learning Processes

Routine Name: Information Foraging/ External Scanning	**Routine Name: Intuiting Routine**

3. Determine topics to scan for like
   (a) Future
   (b) State and federal policy
   (c) Artificial intelligence
   (d) Educational technology
   (e) Content specific
   (f) Demographics and student development
4. On a monthly basis, convene the team to do internet searches. Train the team to look for signals in the designated areas, and save the articles, reports etc. to the Google drive folder.
5. Twice a year, use these meetings to look for any common patterns or strong signals to prepare for.
6. Determine how to share and communicate findings that may impact your school and how you might plan for these.
	3. Have each teacher present their visual or metaphor.
	4. Discuss what similar, underlying patterns emerged.

Routine Name: Interpreting Routine	**Routine Name: Integrating Routine**
Uses: This routine is based on the research on developing *Innovation Configurations* (Hall & Hord, 2011). and can be used at the team level to help develop collective meaning and a shared mental model of the change idea. *Process Steps:* 1. The team lists the specific and essential characteristics or elements of the change idea.	*Uses*: This routine is used at the individual and team level to apply the ideas developed through the creation of the map that interpreted the change idea. 1. The team lists the specific and essential characteristics or elements of the change idea.

Figure 3.4 (Cont.)

Routine Name: Interpreting Routine	Routine Name: Integrating Routine
2. The team now creates descriptions of the different variations of quality for using the change idea. 3. Start with a basic use of the change idea and write descriptions and draw pictures for each element. 4. Next, do the same thing with a growing use of the change idea considering what would be added or done more in-depth. 5. Last, do the same process for optimal usage of the change idea asking what this change idea would look like if it were being used extremely well on an ongoing basis. [Note you can use additional levels to create this map and describe the levels in ways that make sense for your school.] 6. If different teams are working on the same idea, each team's map should be compared and revised to come to a consensus. 7. As you begin to integrate the change idea, use the map on an ongoing basis to guide next steps and to clarify how you define the specific change idea.	2. The team now creates descriptions of the different variations of quality for using the change idea. 3. Start with a basic use of the change idea and write descriptions and draw pictures for each element. 4. Next, do the same thing with a growing use of the change idea considering what would be added or done more in-depth. 5. Last, do the same process for optimal usage of the change idea asking what this change idea would look like if it were being used extremely well on an ongoing basis. [Note you can use additional levels to create this map and describe the levels in ways that make sense for your school.] 6. If different teams are working on the same idea, each team's map should be compared and revised to come to a consensus. 7. As you begin to integrate the change idea, use the map on an ongoing basis to guide next steps and to clarify how you define the specific change idea.

Routine Name: Institutionalizing Routine

Uses: This routine is based on the ideas from the *Levels of Use* (Hall & Hord, 2011) framework and diagnostic. This routine is used to determine how a change idea is taking hold and to determine the varying degrees of use in a building.

Figure 3.4 (Cont.)

Routine Name: Institutionalizing Routine

Process Steps:
1. School leaders and team leaders meet to create the questions for a focused team interview.
2. Questions should focus on determining the depth of knowledge and use of a change idea and should be based on the seven dimensions that compose Levels of Use:
   (a) Knowledge—team's practical and theoretical understanding of the change idea
   (b) Acquiring information—actions taken to seek out information about the change idea
   (c) Sharing—what individuals tells others about the change idea
   (d) Assessing— exploring actual or potential impact of the change idea
   (e) Planning—thinking about next steps for the change idea
   (f) Status reporting—individual's self-report on use of the change idea
   (g) Performing—concrete indicators or behaviors taken
3. Once questions are determined a school or team leader sits down with the team and conducts the interview collecting written notes.
4. Once team interviews are finished, the school and team leaders review the notes looking for patterns or themes related to use and determining next support steps.
5. This routine is used 1–4 times during a year until the leadership feels like the change idea has become institutionalized.

Figure 3.4 (Cont.)

Team Considerations

The 5i model of organizational learning provides a knowledge building and learning container in which all other levels of learning can occur and contribute to capacity development of a school. For many years, organizational learning existed as a nebulous idea with few actionable strategies for school leaders. However, this new model of capacity, which uses the 5i model to explain organizational learning, can give school leaders a deeper understanding and numerous actions to take through the defined routines.

Organizational learning overall is a critical system for operating in the complex environment because it: (1) improves a school's agility; (2) provides faster learning; (3) keeps the school aligned with rapidly changing externalities; and (4) minimizes resource errors.

As we discussed in Chapter 1, schools are complex systems that can learn and change if leaders and leadership teams use the power of social learning and social networks. Over time, emergent ideas and practices happen when adults interact together to create new knowledge around external demands and contextual problems. These interactions are the nature of capacity and help build more capacity over time. As you think more about the organizational learning system and answers on your diagnostic, consider these questions.

1. Now, how are you envisioning capacity in your school?
2. From your perspective, what does it mean when an organization learns?
3. Are there new processes your school needs to learn? Why?
4. What is meant by the content of organizational learning versus the process of organizational learning? Which manages and stores more easily?
5. What does it mean to manage knowledge at a school's organizational level? How and where can knowledge be stored?
6. In the 5i model of organizational learning, which processes might you already be using? Which need more attention?
7. What does it mean to use lean methods?
8. How are Improvement Science and Design Thinking similar? Why might you use one over the other?
9. How can organizational learning processes support or enhance your ideas of school improvement?
10. How are feedback processes used in your school?

References

Bryk, A.S., Gomez, L.M., Grunow, A. and LeMahieu, P.G. (2015). *Learning to improve: How America's schools can get better at getting better.* Harvard Education Press.

Crossan, M.M., Lane, H.W. and White, R.E. (1999). An organizational learning framework: From intuition to institution. *Academy of Management Review,* 24 (3) 522–537.

Hall, G.E. and Hord, S.M. (2011). *Implementing change: patterns, principles, and potholes.* Pearson.

Heifitz, R.A. (1999). *Leadership without easy answers.* Harvard University Press.

IDEO (2012). *Design thinking for educators.* https://designthinkingforeducators.com/

Ismail, S., Malone, M.S. and van Geest, Y. (2014). *Exponential organizations: Why new organizations are ten times better, faster, and cheaper than yours (and what to do about it).* Diversion Books. Kindle Edition.

Jenkin, T.A. (2013). Extending the 4I organizational learning model: Information sources, foraging processes and tools. *Administrative Sciences* 3, 96–109; doi:10.3390/admsci3030096

Krylova, K.O., Vera, D. and Crossan, M. (2016). Knowledge transfer in knowledge intensive organizations: The crucial role of improvisation in transferring and protecting knowledge. *Journal of Knowledge Management,* 20 (5), 1045–1064.

Ortenblad, A. (2018). What does "learning organization" mean? *Learning Organization,* 25 (3), doi:10.1108/TLO-02-2018-0016

Ries, E. (2011). *The lean startup: How today's entrepreneurs use continuous innovation to create radically successful businesses.* Currency.

Senge, P. (2010). *The Fifth Discipline: The Art & Practice of the Learning Organization.* Random House.

Taleb, N.N. (2012). *Antifragile: Things that gain from disorder.* Random House.

Vera, D., Crossan, M. and Apaydin, M. (2011). A framework for integrating organizational learning, knowledge, capabilities, and absorptive capacity. In Easterby-Smith, M. and Lyles, M. (eds), *Handbook of organizational learning and knowledge management,* (2nd edn, 153–180). Wiley.

Capacity as Organizational Conditions

Amanda Lopez had just wrapped her last meeting with her department heads and other teacher leaders in her school and began to review her notes. As she looked at what people had told her about the school, she sensed a deep sense of commitment to the students at Stonybrook High School. She also noticed that the school seemed to be working in twenty different directions at once, with little common focus or vision between teachers and departments. Some departments seemed highly cohesive and were pulling in the same direction, while others seemed like they hardly knew each other. The math department, in particular, seemed like a real team. Their department chair had brought in five other teachers for her meeting with Ms. Lopez to discuss how they had been working to align their vision for math instruction and putting in numerous intervention steps for their students to avoid failure. Their state tests had risen over 14% over the past few years.

In about ten of the interviews, teachers had alluded to the sense that most teachers did not trust the former administrative team and did not feel trusted as professionals. Numerous starts and stops on various initiatives had left teachers with a feeling that nobody knew how to lead the necessary changes. So, most teachers had hunkered down to do the best they could to improve their students' academic outcomes. As she looked at the school's mission statement above her desk, it read, "Excellence in Everything." Ms. Lopez's intuition as a

Capacity as Organizational Conditions

beginning principal told her that many of the conditions she knew were necessary for the successful improvement of schools were not yet in place. They had lots of deep work ahead of them.

Many of the authors discussed in Chapter 2 have found that various conditions lead to enhanced capacity for school improvement and, over time, enhance more exceptional teaching and learning for students (King and Bouchard, 2011). However, without a deep understanding of these conditions and how they help promote learning, school leaders and teams may fail to recognize why proposed initiatives fail. As discussed in Chapter 1, the operating system of a school needs to take on the sophisticated changes necessary to advance learning for all students to a higher level. Again, it is like trying to run a high-powered web-based tool on Windows 95. It just will not work, so a new, more complex code is necessary.

This chapter explores the necessary conditions that need to be in place within a school to support capacity development at all levels of learning. It is the start of the "recoding" that needs developing, so the necessary changes in teaching and learning can occur. In this chapter, we will explore conditions for defining clarity of purpose and instructional guidance, creating coherence, distributing leadership, creating positivity, and knowledge management by explaining what the condition is and essential elements in each (see **Figure 4.1** below). This chapter will also discuss the indicators

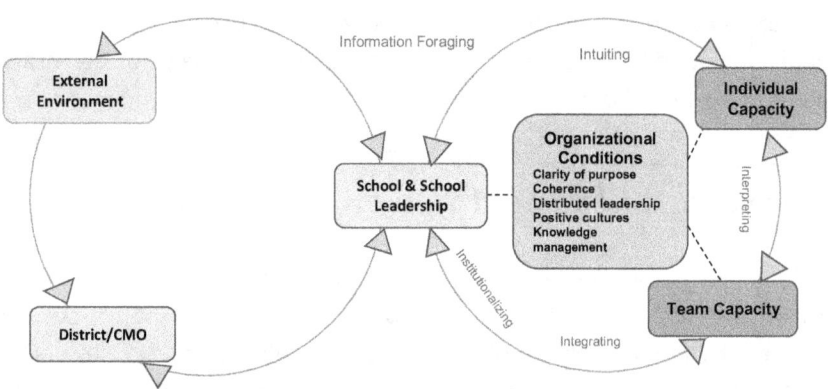

Figure 4.1 Organizational Conditions for Developing Capacity

49

for these conditions and describe the mindsets, skills, and routines leaders can use to develop each.

Organizational Conditions That Support Learning

> Earlier in the summer, Ms. Lopez had been reviewing notebooks left from the previous principal. In one, she found the state-required improvement plan for the past two years. As she read through the plan, she saw a vast number of proposed ideas that were supposed to lead the school toward higher achievement and a better future. However, there didn't seem to be a common thread or purpose behind the proposed strategies, and ongoing adult learning was not addressed. She also could not determine the overall philosophy of the school or if its culture helped support change. It appeared to Ms. Lopez that many of the ideas were solutions in search of a problem, and that these solutions failed to account for the school as an organization.

From the history of public education, it is easy to see that many schools in the United States like change but struggle to improve actual achievement. The constant barrage of new ideas, policies, and programs have left many schools with multiple layers of change sediment in their schools without a real sense of clarity, coherence, or purposeful cultures. To support ongoing learning and knowledge building at the organizational, individual, and team levels, a few critical conditions emerge as necessary in this new model of capacity building.

Condition 1: Clarity of Purpose

All school improvement begins with the role of vision. Vision and mission statements are what Murphy and Torre (2015) refer to as "meaning infusers." Unfortunately, most of these statements do little to develop a cohesive system for clarity of purpose and instructional guidance. In other words, they do not help leaders to infuse meaning or drive direction in their schools.

For example, Schafft and Biddle (2013) in their analysis on school mission statements in one state wrote that:

> Immediately striking to both of us was the relative uniformity across nearly all school district mission statements in terms of their form and content, as well as the repetition of particular themes, regardless of school district location or community context. The mission statements, above all, appeared to be characterized by the repetition of several stock educational tropes. These tropes were often repeated word for word across many statements, such as "life-long learning," preparing students for a "global society," and creating "productive citizens."

By not creating clarity of purpose through purposeful statements and strategies, it is hard for teachers to know where to align their efforts, and loose coupling remains a problem in schools. In Murphy and Torre's (2015) study of practical design and use of vision, mission, and goals in schools, they found when it comes to improving schools, "vision-related activity is the most powerful tool that principals possess." Also, they discovered that vision "acts as the 'organizing principle for work," and that a well-designed and used vision "encourages aligned actions in the service of school improvement" (Murphy and Torre, 2015).

For many generations, the purview of instruction has been left up to the sole discretion of individual teachers (Shen et al., 2017). However, teachers have been left to decide the vision for their classroom without clarity for directing those efforts. As meaning infusers, these statements and how school leaders use them help align school efforts toward something more compelling. Think of the difference a teacher would make if she worked under a mission statement that said, "Excellence in Everything" versus one that stated, "We are an International Baccalaureate school and embrace their ways of instruction." One gives little hope for alignment while the other provides plenty of direction for infusing a teaching staff with meaning.

Besides a compelling purpose, other elements help create this primary system around clarity of purpose. These elements or conditions help promote the purpose and signal to teachers its importance.

Instructional Guidance

First, instructional guidance tools and routines help teachers guide their students by defining more in-depth what needs to be taught, how, and when. Whether a school believes in a traditional time-based form of schooling or a more personalized model, teachers need excellent curriculum and time guidance to know the expectations for learning. In personalized models, students also need guidance tools to know for what they are supposed to be learning.

Academic Press

Second, academic press is a collective condition in which teachers create and hold to high academic and other goal area expectations. This element focuses on the depth and rigor of the academic tasks and learning required of students. The academic press is not a condition of doing more, but a depth and expectations condition set by all teachers and derived from a meaningful vision of learning. Murphy suggests that this academic press does not come from policies or structures put in place but from the "norms of the school as an academic place" (Murphy, 2016). I would also add that schools are becoming more focused on other domains of development that also require a norm of rigor beyond academics.

This element is the basis of the standards movement, but many problems with the rigor of academic work still exist in American schools. For instance, a study done by The New Teacher Project showed that students in the core areas of ELA, math, science, and social studies spent three-quarters of their time on assignments below grade level (TNTP, 2018). In equal terms, students spent six months of critical learning time doing below grade-level work (TNTP, 2018). Time and rigor are two elements under a school's control.

Condition 2: Coherence

The need for coherence as a condition for capacity is critical for two reasons. First, it helps solve the "everybody doing their own thing in their way problem," which creates fragmented learning at all levels. Second, it helps explain the "I am overwhelmed" sense of many leaders and teachers today who have grown weary from initiative after initiative that have piled on top of each other.

Coherence defines as the systematic or logical connections, the integration of diverse elements or relationships, or the quality of forming a unified whole. This definition points to why the clarity of purpose is so important. In many ways, public education has lost credibility for being incoherent or loosely coupled, meaning the parts of the system do not work together in a unified manner around a clear purpose.

From the literature around coherence, three lines of thought have emerged. Early work done on studies in Chicago showed that schools adopt too many unrelated and unconnected programs, projects, and partnerships leading to incoherence in their instructional program when trying to improve (Newmann et al., 2001). Instructional coherence is better for students because more learning occurs when experiences build on and relate to one another, motivation improves when experiences are more linked; and integrated, long-term experiences provide greater clarity for students. In their studies of Chicago schools, these researchers found a strong, positive relationship between improvements in instructional coherence and student achievement (Newmann et al., 2001).

Second, Fullan and Quinn (2016) define coherence more as the degree of integration that exists in a school or system, and the shared depth about the purpose and nature of the work in schools. Like shared mental models, people in schools need to make and remake meaning about their shared purpose continuously. Their framework for coherence centers around simplicity or the smallest number of sensible components that work together for meaning. Their ideas around coherence also discuss these components as the right drivers in a school or system compared to what they call the wrong drivers of focusing on individuals, punitive accountability, technology, and ad hoc policies that can lead to confusion, distrust, and initiative fatigue. Wrong drivers can lead to more complexity and ineffective additions to the learning work of schools.

Third, work by Forman et al. (2017) suggests that, "… they (schools) deliberately create supportive conditions for ordinary educators to engage in systematic and coordinated professional learning that pushes teaching and learning to new and more ambitious levels across classrooms." They define internal coherence as "the collective capability of the adults in a school building or educational system to connect and align resources to carry out an improvement strategy" (Forman et al., 2017). Their ideas on coherence posit that coordinated learning for adults around student learning issues leads to enhanced student learning that leads to better collective efficacy, which further motivates teachers to take responsibility and try new practices.

Condition 3: Distributed Leadership

Research on school leadership utilizes many different perspectives, but many of these perspectives still rely on the heroic model of instructional leadership to lead schools. The great instructional leader is still the holy grail for many schools and systems. In this new model of capacity, however, we take a different perspective using the concept of distributed leadership for several reasons.

First, we believe that the job of leading schools is too complicated for any one individual. Second, to fully understand leadership, it needs to be examined through the perspective of the practice lens or what leaders actually do in their roles (Spillane et al., 2004). Third, from experience, both formal and informal leaders take on various functions and roles to help lead schools. According to Spillane et al. (2004), "... a distributed perspective focuses on how leadership practice is distributed among positional and informal leaders as well as their followers. Understanding how leaders in a school work together, as well as separately, to execute leadership functions and tasks is an important aspect of the social distribution of leadership practice."

According to Harris (2005), three conditions explain the fundamental ideas of distributed leadership:

1. Distributed leadership means focusing on the practice of leadership – which is more important than the function or outcome.
2. Distributed leadership means paying attention to the interactions between people – these are just as important as the actions they undertake.
3. Distributed leadership means acknowledging that situation shapes and influences the form that distributed leadership takes in schools – it may vary according to the context.

Seeing leadership as a practice and set of routines allows school leaders to easily see how this leadership model in their schools could work. Again, distributed leadership frames "leadership practice as a product of the interactions of school leaders, followers, and their situations." Practice takes shape at the intersection of these three elements (Spillane and Camburn, 2006).

Condition 4: Positive Cultures

Beyond all other systems, the system for creating positivity is the foundation for all other conditions in this model. While many ideas about culture and climate abound, schools that focus primarily on creating positivity will make the most significant gains in creating engaging places to learn and work.

All of the ideas in this condition come from the field of positive organizational scholarship, which attempts to show how leaders and organizations can build positive cultures and climates rather than focusing only on their negative aspects. Positive organizational scholarship has shown that more positive organizations help individuals develop toward their higher purpose.

Like other conditions and processes described in this model for developing learning capacity, numerous authors have studied and written about the nature of positive organizations and leadership. For example, Murphy and Seashore-Louis (2018), in their review of the literature around positivity, show that teachers respond better in schools where a positive climate and culture exist guided by positive leadership. They also find that the positive culture condition is one path that helps mediate the relationship between leadership, the organization, and school outcomes.

Quinn (2015) also discusses the centrality of positive cultures for high organizational performance, asking how we move people from being overextended and underutilized to fully engaged and continually renewed? He posits that most people have a regular mental model or set of assumptions for how organizations work: organizations are hierarchies, leadership means a position for directing others, and change driven downward. However, these mental models can be altered to become more positive: organizations are a network of relationships. Leadership means influencing others no matter what their position and that change can emanate from anywhere. Quinn (2015) suggests that organizations are never static and are either becoming more negative or more positive.

To help simplify what could become an overly complicated condition, this model for developing capacity as knowledge building and learning uses Cameron's (2012) factors that help develop a positive cultural system for a school plus one additional.

In our model, the positive cultural condition consists of:

1. *Positive climate*: This is the work environment in which positive emotions dominate over negative ones. Since negative emotions and experiences have a longer-lasting effect on individuals, a focus on positivity is essential. Leaders counter this with an abundance of positivity and the uplifting side of the organization. Developing a positive climate needs to be done intentionally and frequently (Cameron, 2012).

2. *Positive relationships*: These are relationships within the school that are a generative source of enrichment, vitality, and learning. In other words, these are the types of relationships that make people feel better psychologically, physiologically, and emotionally, all of which are essential for learning. Significant relationships have been found to enhance cardiovascular and immune system health, foster greater resiliency, healthier teams, and raise levels of commitment to the organization. Important to note in relationships is that the effects are more significant through giving versus receiving.

3. *Positive communication*: This is the type of communication that uses affirmative and supportive language to replace negative language. Findings suggest that the ratio of positive to negative statements on teams and organizations is the most critical factor in predicting organizational performance (Dutton and Ragins, 2007). These high-performing teams also used more inquiry statements and a focus on others versus self in conversations and connectivity. When corrective or critical messages have to be delivered by leaders, supportive forms of communication must be used to preserve a positive relationship.

4. *Positive meaning*: This factor helps everybody in the school feel like they are pursuing a profound purpose that is personally significant beyond themselves, similar to the section above on clarity of purpose. Even though this seems like a given for helping students succeed, not all people find positive meaning in their work. Finding positive meaning requires that leaders and

cultures help people to see their work as a calling or being driven by the meaning of the work itself rather than rewards or compensation. Positive meaning is developed with individuals when work has: (1) a positive impact on human well-being, (2) an association with a personal value, (3) an impact beyond the immediate, and (4) supportive relationships or sense of community in people (Cameron, 2012). This new model for capacity would add a fifth: Equity for all students.

5. *Positive energy*: While positive energy is not a part of Cameron's primary factors, we believe the concept has merit as part of our model for developing learning capacity. Organizational or positive energy "refers to the force of a collective unit (an organization, department, or team) in pursuit of its goals" (Vogel and Bruch, 2012). These units, which in today's educational environment must continuously adapt and relearn, have to mobilize their energy toward these goals collectively. Positive energy links to enhanced performance, well-being, commitment, collective change, and overall job satisfaction (Vogel and Bruch, 2012).

Bruch and Vogel (2011) extend the notion of positive energy by defining four types found in organizations based on the intensity and quality of expressed energy.

- *Productive energy:* Marked by high emotion and cognitive alertness with high activity, speed, and stamina.
- *Comfortable energy*: Marked by low positive energy, high satisfaction with low activity levels and complacency.
- *Resigned inertia*: Marked by low negative energy with high levels of frustration, withdrawal, cynicism, and low engagement.
- *Corrosive energy*: Marked by high negative energy with aggression and destructive behavior.

In sum, positive energy or highly productive organizational energy is the overt sense people get about the feeling or climate of a school. This state can only be defined as the positive feelings and enthusiasm, cognitive arousal and energy, and dynamic behaviors of pace, intensity and volume people expend toward collective goals and problem-solving.

Condition 5: Knowledge Management

Once knowledge surfaces from an individual or team around a problem of practice, where does that knowledge go? How can it be managed, stored, and shared for others to use? One of the most significant problems in education is that individual teachers and teams continually create impactful knowledge. Yet, there is typically no formal process to store and share this knowledge in most schools. Organizational knowledge is a proven construct and promoted as a key resource and source of competitive advantage in other fields (Vera et al., 2011). Some research has found that knowledge management (KM) can "help achieve the sustainable development of schools" by encouraging teacher sharing, developing teaching practices, and increasing teachers' performance (Cheng et al., 2017). While the overall capacity building model focuses on knowledge building and learning, how schools organize and manage the knowledge created is a condition that can support learning and knowledge building.

Knowledge management is commonly used in knowledge-intensive organizations like schools to improve learning and development. "Knowledge management is a process of organizational practices involving sharing, storing, retrieving and transferring the knowledge possessed by individuals and groups in their daily operations, for pursuing long-term enhanced performance and development of organizations" (Cheng et al., 2017). In short, KM attempts to explain how knowledge is created, disseminated, and stored for ongoing use in organizations.

As a part of learning processes, knowledge management is not considered a separate process but a condition within learning processes. According to Cheng et al. (2017), there are two primary strategies for knowledge management in schools that can help build a knowledge-building culture:

- First, *personalization* is about sharing knowledge through person to person contacts like team meetings or one on one meetings. This strategy attempts to acquire teachers' internal, tacit knowledge and share it in formal and informal modes. Personalization involves the knowledge processes of retrieval, sharing, and use. These ideas are similar to the team learning process described in Chapter 6.
- Second, *codification* is a knowledge management strategy that uses an information technology-based system for storing, retrieving, and

Capacity as Organizational Conditions

applying the knowledge from documents, manuals, visuals, or any other way in which knowledge can be codified and stored. This strategy requires people to codify and store knowledge in a document format that others can retrieve. For example, a school could use Google Drive with separate folders to store and access knowledge.

In sum, knowledge management as a condition interacts significantly with all major learning levels: individual, team, and organizational. This condition is about the degree to which a school leverages knowledge gained, the speed at which it leverages that knowledge, and how that knowledge is managed. This condition ultimately supports a school's knowledge-building strategy and learning processes.

Diagnosing Conditions

> As Ms. Lopez continued over the summer to understand the improvement history of Stonybrook High School, she realized that she would not have time to get a complete history of the school from all of her staff members. She felt that before more improvement and learning could happen, she needed to create the organizational conditions that would help foster the learning processes that would then build capacity in the school. She needed an easier way to diagnose the most important conditions that would enable learning and improvement.

This model of capacity uses the concept of schools as a set of interacting processes for learning to create greater agility and adaptability. For learning to occur at the organizational, team, and individual levels, conditions must be in place to support that learning. Like good soil, water, sun, and temperatures that help crops grow, these conditions can act as the catalyst for more agile knowledge building and learning in schools. For instance, without clarity of purpose, we tend to get lots of changes, but little improvement. Without a clear purpose and processes to determine coherence, improvement processes tend to be scattered. Additionally, without a well-defined routine for knowing what a school needs to improve, team

Capacity as Organizational Conditions

and individual learning cannot be directed toward solving exact problems of practice.

Similarly, since distributed leadership focuses on the critical interdependencies between leaders, followers, and situations, almost all processes in this model for capacity depend on distributed leadership. For instance, effective teams and teaming require other leaders beyond those in formal positions. Formal methods for learning at the organizational level require other leaders as will managing the knowledge gained from this learning.

Last, helping to create positive conditions also requires multiple leaders who carry the vision and culture beyond formal leaders. The condition of a positive organizational culture cannot be mandated but emerges and develops through and with all other conditions and processes to help build the capacity of a school to learn and change over time. While formal leaders have a significant responsibility to create positive meaning and develop positive relationships, all other individuals in a school have the same obligation. Positive energy helps develops the necessary intensity and pace of learning and change.

To get a general sense of the status of these conditions in your school, take a few minutes and take the following diagnostic either individually or as a team.

Organizational Conditions: The school develops and uses conditions to support ongoing learning about external demands and areas for internal improvement.

Conditions at this level of learning	Diagnostic Questions	Responses
		1. Highly inaccurate
		2. Somewhat in accurate
		3. Not sure
		4. Somewhat accurate
		5. Highly accurate
1. Clarity of purpose and instructional guidance	1a. Our purpose as a school gives us clear direction for coordination	1 2 3 4 5

Figure 4.2 Organizational Conditions Diagnostic

Capacity as Organizational Conditions

Conditions at this level of learning	Diagnostic Questions	Responses
	1b. Our school has well defined instructional guidance plans	1 2 3 4 5
	1c. Our improvement or innovation goals have a clear purpose	1 2 3 4 5
	1d. Each area or domain that we teach has a clear vision of success	1 2 3 4 5
	1e. Our school has a strong sense of press for academics and other important outcomes	1 2 3 4 5 Total ____/5=
2. Coherence	2a. We coordinate our learning around a clear direction for improvement.	1 2 3 4 5
	2b. We coordinate our team learning around a clear direction for improvement.	1 2 3 4 5
	2c. Our improvement work has a clear purpose to it	1 2 3 4 5
	2d. Our school aligns its resources with our improvement efforts	1 2 3 4 5
	2e. Teachers develop similar beliefs around our improvement efforts	1 2 3 4 5 Total ____/5=
3. Distributed leadership	3a. Our leadership communicates clear direction for learning	1 2 3 4 5
	3b. Leadership for learning or improvement is shared between principals, teachers and others	1 2 3 4 5
	3c. Other staff members are well prepared to lead learning	1 2 3 4 5
	3d. Others influence me beyond formal leaders	1 2 3 4 5
	3e. Staff member are consistently involved in making decisions about improvement	1 2 3 4 5 Total ____/5=

Figure 4.2 (Cont.)

Capacity as Organizational Conditions

Conditions at this level of learning	Diagnostic Questions	Responses
4. Positive culture	4a. Communication systems promote a flow of information across the entire school	1 2 3 4 5
	4b. The people in our school show compassion toward one another	1 2 3 4 5
	4c. The people in our school are forgiving.	1 2 3 4 5
	4d. The people in our school express gratitude to one another	1 2 3 4 5
	4e. The people in our school have rich relationships with one another	1 2 3 4 5
	4f. The people in our school are very giving to one another	1 2 3 4 5
	4g. The people in our school communicate with lots of affirmation.	1 2 3 4 5
	4h. The people in our school communicate with supportive language	1 2 3 4 5
	4i. Our school feels like it is pursuing a profound vision for our students' futures	1 2 3 4 5
	4j. I feel like we are having a positive impact on students and each other	1 2 3 4 5
	4k. My work has personal meaning to me	1 2 3 4 5
	4l. Our school feels like it has lots of positive energy	1 2 3 4 5
	4m. Our school feels like it directs our discretional energy in the right ways	1 2 3 4 5
	4n. In our school people show up with lots of energy	1 2 3 4 5
		Total ____/14=

Figure 4.2 (Cont.)

Capacity as Organizational Conditions

Conditions at this level of learning	Diagnostic Questions	Responses
5. Knowledge management	5a. Our school has a strong ability to develop a shared understanding of new ideas	1 2 3 4 5
	5b. Once our school accepts an idea, the idea quickly becomes something we use.	1 2 3 4 5
	5c. Once our school accepts an idea, we quickly generate new knowledge from using it.	1 2 3 4 5
	5d. Teachers at our school are good at sharing their deep knowledge of teaching and learning with others	1 2 3 4 5
	5e. We have a common technological system to store and retrieve knowledge and products.	1 2 3 4 5 Total ____/5=

Figure 4.2 (Cont.)

Leading to Create Organizational Conditions

Like needing a basic diagnostic for analyzing the conditions at Stonybrook High School, Ms. Lopez also began wondering about the type of leadership she and other leaders would need to develop to put these organizational conditions in place. She knew from her previous learning and experience that leadership always started with mindsets and skills, but also required actual practices that she could quickly learn and teach to others.

Capacity Model Area	Leadership Mindsets	Leadership Skill(s)
Capacity as Organizational Conditions	• Creating the right conditions for growth • Distributing leadership	1. Developing positivity 2. Strategizing, focusing and prioritizing 3. Crafting purpose with a clear theory of action 4. Designing systems to manage knowledge 5. Developing leadership teams and collaboration 6. Building collective responsibility

Figure 4.3 Leadership Mindsets and Skills for Organizational Conditions

Leadership Mindsets and Skills

To help create the conditions for knowledge building and learning that leads to higher capacity, leaders will need to develop two distinct mindsets. First, both formal and informal leaders need to understand how conditions lay the groundwork for more in-depth learning. Second, leaders need to create a mindset that distributing leadership and sharing power can significantly accentuate the speed and agility of your school's learning. Leadership skills to develop these conditions are listed above and emanate from these two mindsets.

Routines for Organizational Conditions

Five organizational conditions help foster the learning processes at the individual, team, and organizational levels. In-depth guidance is given below on creating instructional coherence and distributing leadership. Routines that help enact the leadership skills for these conditions are also listed below.

Routine Name: **Checking Your Purpose**	Routine Name: **Storytelling for Purpose**
Uses: Once a school's purpose is set, leaders need to know how and if this purpose is being used school wide. This routine can be used as an informal check before a school year begins and mid-way through the year.	*Uses*: This routine can be used to reinforce a school's purpose or elements of purpose.
Process Steps: 1. Using your purpose statement, create a list of the specific elements that lead to that purpose. 2. Create a 4- or 5-point rubric from not apparent to highly apparent on a large sheet and post it. 3. With colored dots, have staff rate how well each element shows up in their classroom and school as a whole. 4. Review the ratings together and discuss ratings and next steps.	*Process Steps*: 1. Review your purpose and elements of purpose at the start of a meeting. 2. Have teachers brainstorm ways that their students have exhibited these elements or ways they have seen others exhibit these elements. 3. Close by examining enhanced meaning of the element.

Routine Name: **Aligning Your Purpose**

Uses: This routine can help teachers reflect on those elements of your school's purpose that they are most aligned to.

Process Steps:
1. Review your purpose and elements of purpose at the start of a meeting
2. Ask teachers to think back over a past period of time (month quarter etc.)
3. Have them reflect on which elements of the school's purpose were most present in their practice and why? Which elements of the school's purpose were least present in their practice and why?
4. Have teachers talk in pairs or small groups about their reflections and possible needs or next steps.

Figure 4.4 Clarity of Purpose Routines

Clarity of Purpose

Clarity of purpose through purposeful statements and strategies is a necessary condition to help teachers know where to align their efforts, and overcome loose coupling in schools.

Instructional Coherence

For coherence, a few crucial elements emerge as necessary to set the overall condition.

1. Similar to the section on the clarity of purpose, it is essential to have a defined purpose or instructional philosophy around which a school can cohere. Coherence builds around the instructional core when driven that way (Newmann et al., 2001).
2. It is essential that opportunities be given to teachers to make sense and meaning out of new learning around and how it connects to the school's defined purpose or instructional philosophy.
3. Frameworks in whatever form are necessary to guide coherence.
4. Professional learning and support need to be primarily around the defined purpose or instructional philosophy of the school and based on student problems of practice within that purpose.
5. Resources of the school primarily need to be allocated toward the school's defined purpose or instructional philosophy.
6. Any potential innovation needs to be analyzed to determine how well it coheres to the school's defined purpose or instructional philosophy. This element suggests schools should still add new innovative outcomes, but once an instructional philosophy is adopted in the core areas, all deliberate attempts should be made to make sure new additions cohere with that philosophy.

Distributed Leadership

While many schools probably distribute leadership now, the need to formally define this system and how it works is necessary for this new model for capacity development. Distributed leadership, like other areas in this model, cannot be forced but emerges from different situations and contexts

Routine Name: **Rigor Walks**	Routine Name: **Coherence Surveys**
Uses: This routine can help leaders gather data around the level of rigor of instruction being done in any one school day. This can be repeated numerous times during the year.	*Uses*: This routine is more qualitative in nature and focuses on gathering data on how any specific process is being used in classrooms.
Process Steps:	*Process Steps*:
1. Create a rubric that determines the rigor of assignments given using any on any number of well-known descriptions.	1. For any specific process create an Innovation Configuration to define and clarify what the process looks like in practice (Hall and Hord, 2011).
2. Create a tracking sheet for each classroom	2. Create a tracking system and schedule for observation
3. On a chosen day using a team of people, do walk throughs in classrooms using the rubric to gauge rigor of work being done and the nature of the work	3. On a chosen day, do walk throughs in classrooms and use the innovation configuration to determine variations in practice
4. Aggregate the findings by rigor level.	4. Aggregate the findings by level.
5. Discuss the implications of findings with staff.	5. Discuss the implications of findings and refine the Innovation Configuration until you have complete agreement on what the process should look like at its optimal use.

Figure 4.5 Instructional Coherence Routines

in which people are allowed to lead. Distributed leadership can happen by default or design, but since it helps foster deeper and richer learning, understanding and designing an effective system is advantageous. The critical steps to create a distributed leadership system include:

1. Creating a *deep understanding* of distributed leadership not as a set of skills, "but as an organizational resource that can be maximized. Distributed leadership means finding and enhancing the sources of formal and informal leadership expertise within and outside the organization" (Spillane et al.,

2015) Understanding distributed leadership is especially crucial for principals who act as formal leads in their schools and may be expected to stay on top of everything. Principals must allow distributed leadership to develop and create the conditions for it to emerge over time. Formal leaders can empower others to lead and provide much-needed energy for change and development. Formal leaders cannot do everything, but they can engage others in the culture and relationships necessary for change.

2. Identify an *organizing schema* for specific leadership functions and practices like instructional leadership, cultural leadership, operational leadership, or cultural leadership and specific routines used for each.

3. Identify *formal leads and backups* for the organizational structure and routines and designing formal networks within the organization. Designating leaders are especially important for content area leadership. Some research suggests that naming a formal subject-specific leadership position "increased the odds of a school staff member being sought out for instructional advice and information within his or her school" (Leithwood, 2016). Content leaders are especially important in large secondary schools where "there is increasing evidence to suggest that more widely distributed patterns of leadership equate with greater potential for organizational change and development" (Spillane and Camburn, 2006).

4. Designing a formal *coordination method* so teams can learn from each other, and formal leaders can have a pulse for movement on goals and need by leadership function. This method includes both coordination and a transparent workflow process based on project management. Formal coordination methods include a regular schedule and rhythm of meetings toward accomplishing set out goals.

5. *Leadership training* for formal leads and backups, so teams and projects add value to the organization and learn how to self-organize (Dignan, 2019). For this element, we are explicitly discussing how to lead productive meetings that look and feel similar throughout the organization. We understand that time for meetings is always limited, so meetings must run well

Capacity as Organizational Conditions

Routine Name: **Creating A Distributed Leadership System**	Routine Name: **Outlining the Learning Year**
Uses: This routine should be done yearly or for new projects to determine how to create the conditions and specifics for distributing leadership.	*Uses*: This routine is used to outline specific timelines reporting deadlines, and feedback loops for projects and school improvement goals.
Process Steps: 1. Study what it means to distribute leadership around functions and tasks investigating co-leading models. 2. Identify the specific functions of leadership that need distributed and shared asking what functions in a school lead to the highest results. 3. Identify the formal leads for each area and their backups. 4. Create a formal coordination method and schedule to enhance the workflow process. 5. Train formal leads and backups in how to run productive meetings.	*Process Steps*: 1. With the leadership team, review all projects and school improvement goals. 2. Using your school calendar, break the year down into manageable chunks e.g. by quarter, every six weeks etc. 3. Using these projects and goals, determine specific benchmarks or key results for each time chunk to accomplish. 4. Map these key results out on a single sheet to share with staff.

Routine Name: **Learning Meetings**

Uses: This routine can be used by your leadership team to create feedback loops and capture key knowledge gained through defined projects and improvement work.

Process Steps:

[Note: many different structures can be used for meetings like these. See for instance www.liberatingstructures.com]

1. Do a brief check in.
2. Have each team or project leader describe what happened on their teams since the last meeting.

Figure 4.6 Distributed Leadership Routines

Capacity as Organizational Conditions

Routine Name: **Learning Meetings**
---

3. Team leaders describe what they have learned about the impact of the project on
   (a) Students
   (b) Staff
   (c) Team
   (d) School culture
4. Group decides which ideas learned should be captured and shared.
5. Group analyzes progress and helps team leader determine ways to plan next steps and strategize for spread.
6. A designated person captures all learning and next steps and shares with whole staff.

Figure 4.6 (Cont.)

and maximize time based on clear purposes that drive the structure and design of the meetings.

6. Last, since leaders emerge from different situations and contexts, understanding and using *co-leading models* have to become explicit.

This model suggests the leader plus aspect of distributed leadership and includes three types:

1. *Collaborated distribution* is carried out by two or more leaders who work in the same place and time to perform the leadership routine, such as when two leaders lead an instructional meeting.
2. *Collective distribution* is carried out by two or more leaders using the same routine but separately and interdependently, for instance, when a principal and a coach give feedback to teachers.
3. *Coordinated distribution* is work that uses activities done in a specific sequence, such as when a principal announces a change and asks team leaders to gather feedback (Spillane and Camburn, 2006).

Routine Name: **Taking the Temperature**	Routine Name: **Developing Relationships**
Uses: This routine is used to gauge the ongoing climate in a building. Instead of doing a climate survey once a year, this simple "flash survey" can be used weekly.	*Uses*: This routine is used to enhance relationships between staff members to help uplift and enrich people. This routine can be used as often as needed.

Process Steps:
1. Create a simple Google form asking 4 simple questions:
  (a) On a scale of 1–10 how positive was your week?
  (b) On a scale of 1–10 how positive were your colleagues this week?
  (c) On a scale of 1–10 how positive was your team this week?
  (d) What would you like to bring to my attention?
2. Have your assistant aggregate the results by individual, school, and team looking for any outliers.
3. Track this data over time and share with staff.
	Process Steps:
	1. Each time you use this routine, have people pair up with a different staff member.
	2. Explain the why behind the routine: To develop stronger relationships to help people feel better psychologically, physiologically and emotionally.
	3. Ask 1–2 questions each time as a way for people to develop stronger relationships. For instance:
	  (a) Who is your hero and why?
	  (b) What is something you have learned recently?
	4. Give each person 1–2 minute to respond and then switch.

Routine Name: **Customizing Your Culture**	Routine Name: **One on One's**
Uses: This routine can be used to help staff members create and internalize positive culture in the school.	*Uses*: To help develop positive relationships, communication and meaning between the school leader(s) and direct reports and to foster improvement through coaching and development of direct reports. Because principals typically have many direct reports, focus on team leaders, instructional coaches and other administrators.

Figure 4.7 Positive Cultures Routines

Capacity as Organizational Conditions

Routine Name: **Customizing Your Culture**	Routine Name: **One on One's**
Process Steps:	*Process Steps*:
1. Explain the role of positive meaning and profound purpose in people's work lives.	1. Establish a monthly scheduled one on one meeting with each direct report
2. Explain that to feel more meaningful and purposeful, a positive culture and sense of community needs to be fostered.	2. Use a shared document and prepare 24 hours in advance of meeting
3. Have staff create three columns on a sheet of paper and work in triads answering these questions in the center column: (a) What gives your work meaning? Why? (b) How does this relate to a personal value of yours? (c) How does your work impact others? (d) How does your work create a ripple effect? (e) How does your work build supportive relationships?	3. Focus the agenda on: (a) Developing interpersonal relationship (b) Information sharing and issues (c) Areas of responsibility and accountability for commitments (d) Team leadership (e) Feedback (f) Development needs and goals (g) Individual needs/obstacles (h) Next action steps
4. On the left side column have the triads list things in schools that detracts from these positive features.	4. Summarize the discussion and next steps on the shared document as a tracking device.
5. On the right-side column have triads list things in the school that adds to or supports these positive features.	
6. Debrief after each step to come to some consensus.	
7. Capture the right-side column ideas and make into an ongoing, featured discussion about culture.	

Figure 4.7 (Cont.)

Routine Name: **Auditing Your School's Energy**	Routine Name: **Creating More Positive Energy**
Uses: This routine is used to gauge the ongoing energy levels in a building. Instead of doing a survey once a year, this simple "flash survey" can be used weekly.	*Uses*: This routine uses the "broaden and build" idea to generate and create more positive energy in a school or team. This routine relies on creating more affective energy, cognitive energy, and behavioral energy.
Process Steps:	*Process Steps:*
1. Create a simple Google form asking four simple questions: (a) On a scale of 1–10 how was your energy level this week? (b) On a scale of 1–10 how was your colleagues' energy level this week? (c) On a scale of 1–10 how was your team's energy level this week? (d) Did you have any energy detractors this week? 2. Have your assistant aggregate the results by individual, school, and team looking for any outliers. 3. Track this data over time and share with staff.	1. At a staff or team meeting ask people to reflect on and share responses to the following: (a) Think about one positive impact of (name a change, new process, part of purpose etc.) you have had recently. (b) When were you most alert to or in tune with (X)? How can you or your team create a collective desire to use or impact (X)? (c) What are some more purposeful behaviors you can take with (X)? How will you do this? 2. Debrief as a staff or team making sure to interject positive praise for the ideas. 3. End by reminding people that positive energy comes from affective energy, cognitive energy, and behavioral energy. Start with small wins to drive your thinking and behavior.

Figure 4.7 (Cont.)

Capacity as Organizational Conditions

Routine Name: **Creating a Knowledge Management Habit**

Uses: This routine should be used as part of team meetings and learning opportunities as a way to capture and share new knowledge.

Process Steps:
1. Create an information storage tool like a shared Google drive.
2. Create folders based on teams, improvement goals, instructional frameworks etc.
3. Create a template for capturing new knowledge. It could have simple sections like:
   (a) Problem or issue
   (b) Context
   (c) Findings or discovery
   (d) Tags
4. Train a select group of people to be knowledge managers whose job it is to capture the knowledge generated by teams or in meetings.
5. Make knowledge capture the summary or last part of every team meeting or learning opportunity.
6. At some designated time period- quarterly for instance- new findings should be collated and shared with staff.

Figure 4.8 Condition 5: Knowledge Management Routines

Positive Cultures

The condition of positivity is the foundation for all other conditions and processes of learning in this model. Schools that develop positive climate, communication, relationships, and meaning will make the most significant gains in creating engaging places to learn and work.

Knowledge Management

How well schools organize and manage the knowledge created through their learning processes can support adaptability and agility. Knowledge management is commonly used in knowledge-intensive organizations but schools will need to create this condition to improve learning and development.

Team Considerations

In sum, one significant aspect of this new model for developing the organizational capacity for learning in schools centers on the conditions, the more implicit aspects of capacity, that can help start the recoding of the school's capacity building processes. These conditions include conditions for clarity of purpose, instructional coherence, distributing leadership, creating positivity, and knowledge management, all with suggested practices and routines to actualize the condition.

As we have previously discussed, school capacity is a complex adaptive system and develops and emerges through the interaction of these conditions with other processes. After taking the diagnostic and reviewing the mindsets and routines, as a team, think more about these conditions and consider these questions.

1. How does your school envision capacity? Why do these conditions matter?
2. Which of these conditions is clearly defined and being used?
3. Does your school have a clear instructional purpose or philosophy around which everything is organized?
4. Does your school have effective instructional guidance systems, and are they being used?
5. Does your school have instructional coherence? What evidence exists?
6. Does your school have a clear plan or design for distributed leadership?
7. Who else can and should "practice" their leadership? Around what tasks?
8. Does your school lean toward a more positive or negative culture?
9. Can others sense the level of energy in your school? How is energy expressed in your school?
10. How is knowledge gained stored and used across your school?

References

Bruch, H. and Vogel, B. (2011). *Fully charged: How great leaders boost their organization's energy and ignite high performance.* Harvard Business Review Press.

Cameron, K. (2012). *Positive leadership: Strategies for extraordinary performance.* Berrett-Koehler Publishers.

Cheng, E.C., Wu, S. and Hu, J. (2017). Knowledge management implementation in the school context: Case studies on knowledge leadership, storytelling, and taxonomy. *Educational Research Policy & Practice* 16, 177–188; DOI 10.1007/s10671-016-9200-0

Dignan, A. (2019). *Brave new work: Are you ready to reinvent your organization?* Portfolio/Penguin.

Dutton, J.E. and Ragins, B.R. (2007). *Exploring positive relationships at work.* Erlbaum.

Forman, M., Leisy-Stocish, E. and Bocala, C. (2017). *The internal coherence framework: Creating the conditions for continuous improvement in schools.* Harvard Education Press.

Fullan, M. and Quinn, J. (2016). *Coherence: The right drivers in action for schools, districts and systems.* Corwin Press.

Hall, G.E. and Hord, S.M. (2011). *Implementing change: patterns, principles, and potholes.* Pearson.

Harris, A. (2005). *Crossing boundaries and breaking barriers: Distributing leadership in schools.* Specialist Schools Trust. www.sst-inet.net

King, M.B. and Bouchard, K.(2011). The capacity to build organizational capacity in schools. *Journal of Educational Administration,* 49 (6), 653–669; doi.org/10.1108/09578231111174802

Leithwood, K. (2016). Department-head leadership. *Leadership and Policy in Schools,* 15 (2), 117–140.

Murphy, J. (2016). *Creating instructional capacity: A framework for creating academic press.* Corwin Press.

Murphy, J.F. and Seashore-Louis, K (2018). *Positive school leadership: Building capacity and strengthening relationships.* Teachers College Press.

Murphy, J. and Torre, D. (2015). Vision: Essential scaffolding. *Educational Management Administration & Leadership,* 43 (2), 177–197.

Newmann, F., Smith, B., Allensworth, E. and Bryk, A. (2001). Instructional program coherence: What it is and why it should guide school improvement policy. *Educational Evaluation and Policy Analysis,* 23 (4), 297–321.

Quinn, R. (2015). *The positive organization: Breaking free from conventional cultures, constraints, and beliefs.* Berrett-Koehler Publishers.

Schafft, K. and Biddle, C. (2013, November). Place and purpose in public education: School district mission statements and educational (dis) embeddedness. *American Journal of Education,* 120, 55–76.

Shen, J. et al. (2017). School as a loosely coupled organization? An empirical examination using national SASS 2003–2004 data. *Educational Management Administration & Leadership,* 45(4) 657–681; DOI: 10.1177/1741143216628533 journals.sagepub.com/home/ema

Spillane, J.P. and Camburn, E. (2006). *The practice of leading and managing: The distribution of responsibility for leadership and management in the schoolhouse.* Paper presented at the Annual Meeting of the American Educational Research Association, San Francisco, April 7–11, 2006.

Spillane, J.P., Halverson, R. and Diamond, J.B. (2004). Toward a theory of leadership practice: A distributed perspective. *Journal of Curriculum Studies,* 36 (1), 3–34; doi: 10.1080/0022027032000106726

Spillane, J. Hopkins, M. and Sweet, T. (2015). Intra- and interschool interactions about instruction : Exploring the conditions for social capital development. *American Journal of Education,* 122 (1), 71–110. Doi 10.1086/683292

TNTP (2018). *The opportunity myth: What students can show us about how school is letting them down – and how to fix it.* https://opportunitymyth.tntp.org

Vera et al. (2011). A framework for integrating organizational learning, knowledge, capabilities, and absorptive capacity. In Easterby-Smith, M., Lyles, M. (eds), *Handbook of organizational learning and knowledge management,* (2nd edn, 153–180). Wiley.

Vogel, B. and Bruch, H. (2012). Organizational energy. In Cameron, K.S. and Spreitzer, G.M. (eds) *The Oxford handbook of positive organizational scholarship.* Oxford University Press, 691–702.

Capacity as Individual Skills and Beliefs

> Amanda Lopez finally made it back to her office after a long day of observations and feedback. As a first-year principal, she had made a vow to try and spend 50% of her week in this vital work of instructional leadership but was falling short of her goal. While she felt good about designing and carrying out whole group presentations for the staff at Stonybrook High School, she wondered why the techniques that had been shared were not showing up in all of the classrooms. As a teacher, she was a willing and motivated learner who always wanted to try new ideas for the benefit of her students. Not that all of the ideas always made sense for her, but she was innovative and curious enough to modify them for her purposes. Amanda Lopez was a curious learner at heart, but as she reviewed her notes and conversations, she could tell that was not the typical pattern for many of her teachers. Some took on none of the ideas; some took on surface-level components, and some dug deeply into their practice to see how the new ideas could fit. As the clock ticked past 5:30, she began to wonder how to understand why this had happened and what she could do about it.

We have now explored the conditions and processes that can lead to knowledge building and learning in the school organization. This chapter turns to learning and developing expertise at the individual level. Teacher learning and developing their expertise needs to be the central focus of

Capacity as Individual Skills and Beliefs

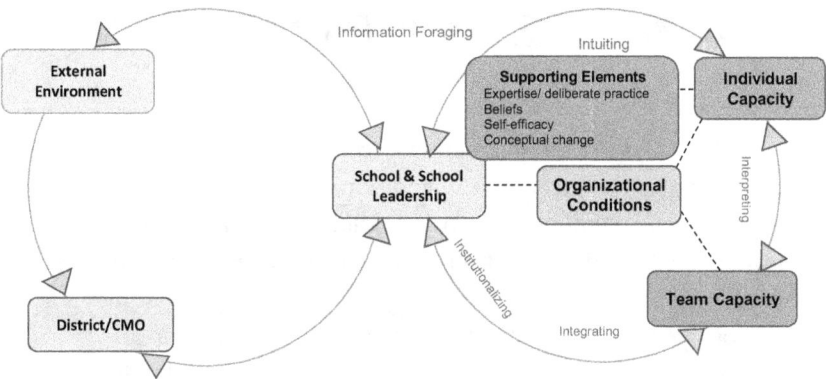

Figure 5.1 Elements that Support Individual Capacity for Learning

capacity building. Just like the education field has begun to understand the role of motivation and emotions in student learning, leadership in a high capacity school also recognizes the role of motivation and emotions in individual teacher learning. In short, high capacity schools embrace the idea that whole group professional learning is just the start of learning for teachers, and that other models have to be used based on individual needs. In a world of personalized learning for students, schools need to include personalized learning for adults.

To not lose the central thread of this book, take a moment, and review what this book is attempting to define more clearly.

Capacity as a noun means the set of defined processes and conditions that help a school organize for learning at the individual, team, and organizational level within a central purpose. Over time, this learning becomes a resource that can be drawn upon to improve agility and adaptability.

Capacity Development as a verb means using processes to promote interaction for learning at the individual, team, and organizational level to build more dynamic agility and adaptability.

This chapter will explore individual teacher learning and growth in the Intuiting and Interpreting phases of organizational learning explored in Chapter 3 (see **Figure 5.1** above). This chapter also examines four elements that support individual learning capacity. All of these elements have implications for leaders' work in building knowledge in their schools and the routines they use to help individuals learn.

The Role of Beliefs in Teacher Learning

> From her days as an instructional coach and assistant principal in working with teachers, Ms. Lopez realized that no matter how effective her communication or modeling was, teachers sometimes heard something different. Even when she would have teachers practice a new skill with her, they would often revert to what they had previously done. Recently she had started to wonder if something deeper than cognitive understanding was at play during her feedback sessions.

Without debate, Ms. Lopez is discovering that beliefs are a large part of teachers and their enacted teaching. Teachers hold belief systems about the nature of their knowledge, students in general, some students in particular, their pedagogy, their identities, and what they believe they can accomplish. Some of these beliefs form early in a teacher's life and some early in their career. Some may modify over time, and some may hold steady throughout a teacher's career. To support individuals in their knowledge building, this new model of capacity suggests that leaders must understand what beliefs are, how they develop and change, and their importance in developing excellent teaching. If a model of capacity does not focus on teacher beliefs, compliance may occur but only at a surface level.

What are Beliefs?

A fundamental view suggests that beliefs are the stories we tell ourselves to define a personal sense of reality (Uso-Domenech and Nescolarde-Selva, 2016). Beliefs arise through our experiences and form a nested interrelationship that forms together into a belief system. Belief systems help us make sense of our experiences and the world in which we live and do not have to be based in reality as long as they provide an adequate explanation (Uso-Domenech and Nescolarde-Selva, 2016). New experiences or ideas are assimilated or rejected through the filters of our belief systems and get reinforced by the cultures in which we live and work. Beliefs also "represent an individual's representation of reality or what an individual holds to be true, whether or not evidence supports that representation. Beliefs have enough personal validity and credibility to guide behavior and thought" (Fives and Buehl, 2016).

Shermer (2011) asserts that

> we form our beliefs for a variety of subjective, personal, emotional and psychological reasons in the context of environments created by family, friends, colleagues, culture, and society at large; after forming our beliefs, we then defend, justify and rationalize them with a host of intellectual reasons, cogent arguments and rational explanations. Beliefs come first, explanations for beliefs follow. I call this process belief-dependent realism, where our perceptions about reality are dependent on the beliefs that we hold about it. Reality exists independent of the human mind, but our understanding of it depends upon the beliefs we hold at any given time.

Belief systems of all humans have certain qualities and characteristics. For this system of individual capacity, some critical features include:

- People have a personal commitment to their belief systems. Many teachers, for instance, have committed to working with and serving children as the next generation.
- Belief systems vary infinitely in their content by different people. Given the complexity of teaching and learning, some teachers may have a deep belief about certain aspects like how students enter a classroom, whereas others may have never considered it.
- Belief systems vary in their complexity by different people. Some teachers think deeply about their craft and reflect on their strategies and actions, while others may not.
- Belief systems may be, in part, concerned with the existence or non-existence of certain concepts. For instance, education is ripe with practices that do not exist in the research literature but have remained in the lexicon and practice of many people like learning styles.
- Belief systems carry a substantial amount of episodic material. Teaching by nature is highly episodic, and therefore, most of a teacher's beliefs develop from these episodes. A teacher has a conflict with a female student and begins to believe that females are harder to teach than males.

- Belief systems hold with varying degrees of certitude (Uso-Domenech and Nescolarde-Selva, 2016). For teachers, some beliefs like those about students may be immovable, while others like pedagogical beliefs may be less certain.

Relative to teachers and teaching, various ways have been used to describe the nature of teachers' beliefs. Teacher beliefs usually center around pedagogy, knowledge, and students as learners (Fives and Buehl, 2016). Teachers hold views related to the nature, purpose, and methods of teaching and shape their practice by these beliefs. These beliefs are the basis for many changes and central to many reform efforts. Similarly, beliefs about the nature of knowledge also shape a teacher's work. The nature of knowledge for teachers centers on "(a) certainty of knowledge (as unchanging or fluid), (b) simplicity of knowledge (as isolated or interconnected), (c) source of knowledge (from an external authority or constructed by the self), and (d) justification of knowledge (the processes and evidence needed to evaluate knowledge claims" (Fives and Buehl, 2016).

Finally, teachers hold varying beliefs about the students they teach and profoundly influence what students are taught. A teacher's beliefs about students generally focus on their abilities and the choices a teacher makes about instructional and curriculum practices. These choices have been linked to a teacher's mindset, which varies by age, experience level, and content area (Fives and Buehl, 2016). Teachers with growth mindsets tend to be more "supportive of students, teach explicit problem-solving skills, and are open to information about change." In contrast, teachers with fixed mindsets tend to be "less supportive and implement practices that reduce engagement" (Ratta et al., (2012).

A teacher's belief system can come from a variety of sources, experiences, and perspectives. Like all other humans, teachers take new ideas and experiences and often unknowingly through their brains,

> filter them through colored lenses of worldview, paradigms, theories, hypotheses, conjectures, hunches, biases, and prejudices accumulated through living. We then sort through the facts and select those that confirm what we already believe and ignore or rationalize away those that contradict our beliefs.
>
> (Shermer, 2012)

Self-efficacy

> When she was a teacher, Ms. Lopez always had confidence that she could learn something new about her practice and work on perfecting it over time. She always believed that she could find ways to make all of her students love her class and subject. As Ms. Lopez had been working with new teachers, she noticed many of them did not have that same confidence and started to blame students. She began to hear more of the, "I tried, but they just don't care" attitude. Ms. Lopez knew that part of her work and the work of other leaders needed to be around building a more agile, confident set of beliefs in her younger teachers.

One significant belief teachers hold bases in their self-efficacy. With numerous teachers leaving the profession yearly because they do not feel efficacious in their chosen profession, helping teachers develop this important belief is a necessary element of individual capacity that must grow at the personal level.

The underlying origins of this concept come from Bandura's (1977) theory of self-efficacy. The theory of self-efficacy posits that ongoing cognitive processes play an essential role in acquiring, changing, and maintaining new behaviors in humans. In accordance, self-efficacy theory suggests that people possess outcome expectancies for their actions like success or failure. People tend to avoid threatening situations that exceed their ability to handle them to avoid failure, and in contrast, accept situations where they judge they can feel successful. These self-generated expectations or "efficacy expectations determine how much effort people will expend and how long they will persist in the face of obstacles and aversive experiences" (Bandura, 1977).

The information for these expectations of self-efficacy comes from four sources of information:

- *Performance accomplishments*: Ongoing success on tasks or behaviors raises mastery expectations while repeated failure lowers them, especially early in the behavior change. Once strong efficacy builds through repeated success, occasional failures tend not to diminish the efficacy expectation.

Capacity as Individual Skills and Beliefs

- *Vicarious experiences*: Seeing other teachers perform some change successfully without adverse consequences can also generate positive, mastery expectations for improvement with persistent efforts.
- *Verbal persuasion*: In this source of information, people are persuaded or convinced that they can handle the change effort to change the efficacy expectation. Although this is a common form of information between leaders and teachers, efficacy expectations raised this way tend to be lower because they do not provide an authentic experience for the teacher.
- *Emotional arousal*: Last, emotions rising from new performance expectations raise stress and signal teachers that the degree of anxiety felt is also robust information concerning personal efficacy (Bandura, 1977).

In general, Bandura's research showed that the higher the increments in self-perceived efficacy, the more significant the changes in behavior. His theory posits that for teachers to feel efficacious, they process and integrate various information concerning their capability for a change idea, and they regulate behavior and effort accordingly (Bandura, 1977).

Other researchers took Bandura's theory and applied it specifically to the self-efficacy of teachers and teaching. They defined teacher efficacy as the "extent to which the teacher believes he or she can affect student performance" (Tschannen-Moran et al., 1998). These authors extended Bandura's work by suggesting that a teacher's self-efficacy has two different forms of expectation. First is the efficacy expectation in which an individual has the conviction he or she can perform a specific task. The second is the outcome expectation in which an individual estimates the likely consequence of performing at an expected level. In other words, self-efficacy is specific to a particular task and one's self-perception of competence versus their actual skill. For instance, a teacher may feel very productive in teaching an intermediate grade level, but if asked to change to a primary grade, it may not feel as efficacious.

In their self-efficacy model, Tschannen-Moran et al. (1998) keep the same sources of efficacy information but add cognitive processing about analyzing the teaching task and assessing one's teaching competence as other factors that lead to teacher efficacy and performance. They also suggest that when tasks are new, salient or important, teachers tend to engage in more rigorous analysis, but that during change, teacher's perceived efficacy tends to lag behind their performance. During these changes, verbal persuasion is an essential source of efficacy information and can boost effort if the person giving the feedback is considered credible, trustworthy, and has expertise. Without these qualities, feedback may lower a teacher's efficacy. These authors also propose that collaboration with peers tends to increase vicarious experiences and verbal persuasion sources of information and help create a virtuous cycle of change (Tschannen-Moran et al., 1998).

Why Self-Efficacy is Important to Consider

When leaders work to understand how to develop individuals' capacity, self-efficacy is a seemingly basic idea with huge implications. As explored, how individual teachers judge their abilities to impact student outcomes has consistently correlated with teacher behavior, student attitudes, and student achievement (Tschannen-Moran and Hoy, 2001). Efficacy affects the effort they invest in teaching, the goals they set, and their level of aspiration (Wang et al., 2015). Teachers with a strong sense of efficacy tend to plan more, give more effort, and find ways to help their students.

A more critical type of outcome expectancy for teachers in the twenty-first century is for learning to teach in new ways, use of new curricula, and embrace different outcomes with which they have little or no skill. Despite occasional use of the term "teachers' efficacy beliefs," the research described above does not focus on specific efficacy beliefs (e.g., "I can teach new effective writing," or "I can effectively use blended learning"). Nor did any of this research consider the potential fluctuations of teacher efficacy over different time spans (e.g., "hourly, daily, weekly, monthly, and or yearly considerations in understanding teacher efficacy" (Liou et al., 2019). Increasing self-efficacy is not a straight trajectory upwards. It may constantly adjust during change efforts as many individuals face an "implementation dip" in self-efficacy when teachers face new challenges and plateaus during these initiatives. According to Liou et al. (2019)

> ... schools and school leaders need to pay attention to understanding teachers' beliefs about whether they think they are able to do so (implement new ideas), whether they perceive sufficient resources that support them in this endeavor,

and the degree to which they believe doing so would make a positive impact on their teaching and student learning. Notably, teachers' self-efficacy beliefs are the most influential among all beliefs constructs on their actions.

Conceptual Change

> During small group meetings and one on one feedback sessions, Ms. Lopez had started to notice what she labeled as the "processing pause." After she suggested a new technique with students, some of her teachers would pause for long periods. Ms. Lopez felt that she could almost see the wheels spinning as teachers grabbled with the ideas. She began to think that they were thinking about much more during those pauses than her suggestions.

In the increasingly complex world, many of the reform ideas suggest more complex learning, interrelationships of concepts, and sophisticated practices for teachers. How teachers respond to these reform ideas depends on ongoing decisions teachers make during planning, instruction, and assessment, reflecting their underlying beliefs about the nature of learning, knowledge, and students' abilities (Fives and Buehl, 2016).

Teachers often use a heuristic to make these decisions based on their "beliefs to filter new information, frame salient tasks, and guide action" (Fives and Buehl, 2008). Responsible for implementing these new ideas, all teachers hold beliefs that can support or undermine how learners experience these new ideas in their classrooms. Therefore, for any new ideas related to a teacher's practice, leaders must consider their beliefs and support their development.

Change in practice requires that individuals try and deliberately practice new thinking and actions which require accommodations to beliefs and concepts held about teaching and learning. To help teachers develop their capacity for ongoing learning and change, school leaders need to understand not only beliefs and self-efficacy, but also how these two significant elements can help inform the process by which teachers accept or reject new ideas. The Cognitive-Affective Model of Conceptual Change (CAMCC) (Gregoire, 2003) centers around how teachers change their

Capacity as Individual Skills and Beliefs

beliefs and suggests that teachers use cognitive and affective processing when accepting new ideas.

Here is how the model works in brief.

1. First, a reform message presents to a teacher in a specific situation. The message has to be explicit enough in its principles so that the teacher questions what they are doing relative to this idea.

2. If strong enough, this message may threaten the person's teaching identity, so they implicate themselves negatively or positively around the idea. If the teacher believes they are already using the concept, they make a benign positive appraisal because they lack the motivation to investigate or process the idea in more depth. This positive appraisal is when the "I already do this" type of response rises.

3. This positive appraisal serves as a cue to use regular processing to compare the new idea to the teacher's current practice. In general, this type of processing stays at the surface level of both the change idea and the teacher's current practice.

4. The next step is a decision in which a teacher decides to yield to the idea. If they do yield or accept the idea, it assimilates into old beliefs, which leads to only superficial change. If yielding does not occur, there is no change in belief structure or practice.

5. In contrast, going back to Step 2, if teachers do implicate themselves or know they are not genuinely using the new idea, they go through anxiety, causing a stress reaction and an appraisal of the stress. This anxiety often happens implicitly, with the teacher feeling that she may not be doing everything they can to help their students.

6. To relieve anxiety, teachers appraise this stress to determine if they have the motivation, self-efficacy, and capacity to take on the idea. In other words, the stress appraisal causes them to go through both an affective and cognitive judgment of themselves and their motivation and abilities to learn something new in their practice.

7. If the teacher does not feel like they can meet the demands, they label the change idea as a threat and work to avoid the change

using the same regular processing discussed in Step 3. This decision is similar to a fixed mindset in that the teacher does not believe they have the motivation, skills, or support to make the change. Many coping mechanisms appear at this stage to help protect the teacher's overall ego and identity.

8. If the teacher does feel sufficient to meet the changing demand, they appraise the change as a challenge and use an approach intention similar to a growth mindset. The teacher believes that with the right level of effort, practice, and support, they can master the new idea or skill.

9. The teacher then does more systematic processing of the idea in comparison to their current practice. A major tenant of this model is that significant, lasting belief change cannot occur without teachers systematically processing the reform message (Gregoire, 2003). This step is where good professional learning is critical to help teachers do the hard but necessary work of processing and practicing the change idea.

10. After systematically processing the reform ideas, teachers still have to yield or fully accept the idea. If they do, actual conceptual change will occur after more intensive professional learning and practice with the ideas. This professional learning may take years.

The teachers who use an avoidance intention but yield because of some other pressure are why many reform ideas do not profoundly change the look of US classrooms. Teachers will often take one element of the reform idea and show how they embrace the reform ideas. For instance, in a balanced literacy initiative, many teachers take the traditional read-aloud approach and say they were doing shared reading. Alternatively, a high school math teacher who has students use calculators to find the right answers but say they embrace problem-solving ideals may only be processing it at a surface level. Change often threatens teachers' identity, and this model helps leaders see how powerful the human mind is at assimilating these ideas into current beliefs about teaching, students, and knowledge.

In sum, whether teachers take on and use new reform ideas is dependent on both cognitive and affective appraisal of the original idea. Teachers who have high self-efficacy tend to see the ideas as a challenge and work to make sense of them. Others who believe they are already using the approach or who have low self-efficacy see the ideas as a threat and find ways to avoid deep processing of the methods to prevent an implication of their skills and to protect their identity as a teacher.

Expertise and Deliberate Practice

> In her spare time, Amanda Lopez was an avid piano player. At one point, she had considered becoming a concert pianist but felt drawn to work with children. Through her many years of practice, Ms. Lopez had developed a belief that intentional and deliberate practice in any field could create expertise. In her career as a teacher, she carried this belief into her classroom, letting students know she was working on a new technique to help them or a new part of the curriculum to see how they would respond. Amanda would ask for their input and feedback to adjust and deepen her practice. With this experience, she wondered how she could create a practice mentality with her teachers.

In any human endeavor, people spread across a continuum from novice to expert. The same is true for teachers and teaching. The quality of expertise is needed for all teachers, no matter what grade or subject they may teach. Many suggest that the focus on developing expertise is the quality missing in many of the current reform or school improvement ideas (Markholt et al., 2018). These authors suggest that the increased focus solely on evaluation and evaluation quality may give more reliable ratings of teacher quality. Still, it leaves out the essential question of how to improve teaching. This question is the heart and soul of capacity: how school leaders can create the conditions and processes so that teachers are always growing and moving past the edge of their current competence. The answer to this requires enlightened leadership and stable routines based on developing expertise in teachers.

So, what is expertise? Expertise defines as the "characteristics, skills, and knowledge that distinguish experts from novices or less experienced people" (Erricsson, 2006) In complete detail, experts are known by their abilities to:

- Generate the best solutions, faster and more accurately than others.
- Detect and see features and see the deep structure of a situation that a novice cannot.
- Analyze a problem by using domain-specific knowledge and general constraints in their domains of expertise.
- Self-monitor or detect errors in their understanding more effectively.
- Choose the appropriate strategies to handle situations more successfully.
- Choose and use information or resources opportunistically while solving problems.
- Retrieve relevant domain knowledge and strategies with less cognitive effort.
- Organize their understanding of content, pedagogy, and students in highly efficient and organized ways (Chi, 2006).

Think about the best teacher you have had, worked with, or seen. All of these abilities probably come to mind. While expert teachers possess all of these qualities plus in-depth content and pedagogical knowledge, much of the experts' knowledge is tacit and hard to explain.

The Role of Deliberate Practice

To understand how expertise develops, leaders need to understand the difference between routine and adaptive expertise (Bransford et al., 2005). Routine experts develop a set of core competencies that lead to greater efficiency over time. In contrast, adaptive experts change their core competencies and "expand the breadth and depth of their expertise" (Bransford et al., 2005). In teaching, a routine expert is highly efficient and would be considered a reliable teacher but may struggle when deeper or newer pedagogical ideas appear.

In contrast, an adaptive expert is willing to lose a bit of efficiency to learn and practice a new pedagogy. These teachers are more able to let go of previous beliefs, tolerate ambiguity, and rethink what they are doing. Thinking about the development of individual teachers and how leaders help teachers move from being a novice to an apprentice to a routine expert to an adaptive expert is critical for high-capacity organizations.

Many studies have shown that teachers tend to plateau with their skill level after a few years, with many becoming routine experts (Bransford 2005). After this time, teachers tend not to grow or gain new skills and knowledge. However, the complexity in the craft of teaching requires an ongoing and intentional focus on development. As research finds more about learning, student challenges, and the requirements of a new era, teachers must be continually open and willing to become adaptive experts.

So how do teachers develop into adaptive experts? We know that the traditional forms of professional learning may help build new knowledge but do little to enhance the skill in practice. Instead, what is needed is a more robust approach to learning called "deliberate practice" (Ericsson and Pool, 2017). Because educators have all spent so much time learning in classrooms, the institutional belief is that this type of training easily translates into the actual act of teaching. While this form of learning may give teachers more knowledge, most cannot and do not shift this into changes in practice. Experts in this area suggest, only "the right sort of practice carried out over a sufficient period leads to improvement. Nothing else" (Ericsson and Pool, 2017).

Diagnosing Individual Learning Elements

Understanding and developing capacity in a school again requires taking a systems perspective to show how various levels of learning and their elements interact in a mutually supportive and reciprocal manner. For example, expertise in teaching comes not just from experience but a clear purpose of growing individual expertise through capable teams and processes.

Similarly, the element of beliefs and self-efficacy will grow in a school when a clear purpose exists along with a team that helps builds a teacher's belief system and sense of efficacy in a real teaming situation that exhibits psychological safety for exploration of new ideas.

When it comes to the work of teachers' conceptual change around a new idea, again, supportive teams and systems of development and support are highly necessary. Also, how the original idea links conceptually to the school's defined purpose and instructional guidance system will help support teachers during change.

To get a general sense of the status of these elements that support individual learning in your school, take a few minutes, and consider

Capacity as Individual Skills and Beliefs

Individual Learning Level: The school develops the necessary elements and routines to support ongoing individual learning about external demands and areas for internal improvement.

Elements at this level of learning	Diagnostic Questions	Responses 1. Highly inaccurate 2. Somewhat inaccurate 3. Not sure 4. Somewhat accurate 5. Highly accurate
1. Beliefs and mental models	2a. Our school has explicitly addressed the roles of beliefs in teaching and learning.	1 2 3 4 5
	2b. Our school develops the beliefs about new ideas and shares these with teachers.	1 2 3 4 5
	2c. Our school frequently addresses beliefs about new ideas during learning phases.	1 2 3 4 5
	2d. Individuals and teams recognize their biases when learning about new ideas.	1 2 3 4 5
		Total ____/4=
2. Self-efficacy	3a. Our school explicitly addresses the role of self-efficacy in addressing new ideas.	1 2 3 4 5
	3b. When developing learning opportunities our school considers various ways to develop self-efficacy.	1 2 3 4 5
	3c. During learning and change efforts, our school tries to determine levels of self-efficacy.	1 2 3 4 5

Figure 5.2 Individual Learning Capacity Diagnostic

Capacity as Individual Skills and Beliefs

Elements at this level of learning	Diagnostic Questions	Responses
	3d. Our leaders try to intervene when low self-efficacy is evident in teachers.	1 2 3 4 5
		Total ____/4=
3. Conceptual change models	4a. Our school uses a specific conceptual change model when introducing new ideas.	1 2 3 4 5
	4b. At our school new ideas are presented with enough detail for teachers to process.	1 2 3 4 5
	4c. Our school uses a systematic processing method to help teachers compare the new idea to their current practice.	1 2 3 4 5
	4d. Our school is good at recognizing the affective dimension of accepting new ideas.	1 2 3 4 5
		Total ____/4=
4 Expertise and deliberate practice	1a. Our school has an explicit way to determine expertise with new ideas or innovations	1 2 3 4 5
	1b. Our school has an explicit way to determine if people are plateauing in their growth around new ideas or techniques	1 2 3 4 5
	1c. Our school has a process to create deliberate practice for teachers around new ideas or innovations	1 2 3 4 5
	1d. Our school has explicit ways to support the growth of individuals toward expertise.	1 2 3 4 5
		Total ____/4=

Figure 5.2 (Cont.)

Capacity as Individual Skills and Beliefs

the following individual learning capacity diagnostic individually or as a team.

Leading to Create Individual Capacity

> Amanda Lopez knew that with such a large staff, there was no conceivable way that she could personalize teacher learning and work with every teacher by herself. She recognized that from a distributed perspective, all of her leadership team members and teacher leaders would need to understand how to lead and develop others and be willing to be led and developed by others. She also recognized that everybody in her school would need to be both teacher and learner, depending on the situation.

Leadership Mindsets and Skills

To help create individual learning capacity, all leaders will need to develop two new mindsets. First, leaders will need to become highly attuned to recognizing insights that people make about new ideas and spreading them to others. Second, a growth mindset will also be essential as leaders work with others' belief systems and help develop individuals' efficacy.

Capacity Model Area	Leadership Mindsets	Leadership Skills
2. **Intuiting (individual learning)**	• Recognizing insights • Growth mindset	1. Working with beliefs and clarifying mental models 2. Leading systematic processing 3. Influencing efficacy 4. Noticing hidden patterns

Figure 5.3 Leadership Mindsets and Skills for Individual Learning

Leadership skills to develop these conditions are listed below and emanate from these two mindsets.

Routines for Individual Learning Capacity

Both formal and informal leaders need to recognize the influence of four interacting elements that can lead to deeper individual learning. Routines that can be used for each of these elements are described below.

Element 1: Beliefs

To deeply understand the belief system of a teacher and help them develop, leaders must consider

- What people value in teaching and learning?
- What are their substantive beliefs about students, pedagogy, and knowledge?

Routine Name: **Creating Mental Models**

Uses: Over time as individuals practice a specific set of sub skills, they will start to develop a mental model of expert performance. This routine can be used to help develop a more robust collective mental model around a change idea. Use this routine on a team or with an entire staff.

Process Steps:
1. Review the Innovation Configuration (Hall and Hord, 2011) of the change idea being worked on.
2. Have individuals analyze their performance against the descriptions.
3. Have individuals discuss exemplars and non-exemplars and note newly emerging features of the process or steps that make it exemplary. (Note: you are looking to see if people are getting more nuanced in the ways they are discussing the descriptors. You are also looking for common errors or misconceptions.)
4. Guide the teams or individuals in creating new thoughts and language around the change idea adding or revising the Innovation Configuration.

Figure 5.4 Beliefs Routines

Capacity as Individual Skills and Beliefs

Routine Name: **Creating Self-Efficacy**	Routine Name: **Changing Your Inner Narrative (Andersen, 2019)**
Uses: This routine uses the sources of information from which teachers develop self-efficacy to help individuals develop a sense of accomplishment. This routine can be done one on one or with teams, and can be used on an on-gong basis to open or close conversations to help create more self-efficacy.	Uses: To help build individual efficacy, build self-awareness, and focus on growth opportunities. This simple routine can be used in group or individual situations.
Process Steps: 1. A team leader or administrator opens with a review of the change happening and why it is important to reflect and review successes. 2. Have individuals reflect on and list successes they have had with new change ideas and their impact on students. 3. Have individuals share their accomplishments (note this step is using the information source as performance accomplishments as well as hearing others' accomplishments can lead to vicarious experiences—another information source). 4. The team leader or administrator then describes successes they have seen (again using vicarious experience information sources). 5. Last the team leader or administrator discusses positive effort of individuals and how they are handling the changes (again using verbal persuasion and emotional arousal as information sources).	*Process Steps*: 1. Explain that our self-talk is often what inhibits our abilities to make meaningful progress in our practice. 2. Give examples of unsupportive self-talk • I don't need to learn this • I'm already fine at this • This is boring • I'm terrible at this 3. Ask these more supportive questions and have individuals write down their responses • What would my future look like if I did learn this? • Am I really fine at this? How do I compare with others? • I wonder why others find it interesting. • I'm making beginner mistakes, but I'll get better. 4. Have individuals reflect on their responses and how pre and post responses can help develop a growth mindset.

Figure 5.5 Self-Efficacy Routines

Capacity as Individual Skills and Beliefs

Routine Name: **Presenting New Ideas**	Routine Name: **Systematic Processing**
Uses: This routine can be used when discussing or introducing new ideas or methods to try in teaching. This process helps people begin to think about the cognitive and emotional accommodations in the new idea.	Uses: Once a new idea has been presented and processed at a surface level, people will need a more through or systematic way to process the proposed change idea. This process can help people develop a deeper sense of the change idea and how it compares to their current practice.
Process Steps:	*Process Steps*:
1. A school or team leader proposes a new idea for improvement. 2. The specifics of the idea are explained (e.g. *This change idea is about … or This change idea will require …* 3. Participants then rate their stress level and discuss *This idea will be a threat to me. 1–5* *This idea will be a challenge to me 1–5* 4. Participants then think about their motivation to taken on the new idea *I believe with the right supports, I can be successful with the new idea. 1–5* 5. Participants then discuss what kind of time, knowledge, support, and resources they will need to be successful. 6. The school or team leader than captures the general consensus from the questions and discussions of the group.	1. Prior to using this process, the school leader, team leaders or some leadership group unpacks the change idea and lists the specific elements of the change idea that are required for fidelity (Note: team can use the Innovation Configuration tool presented in Chapter 3.) 2. Once the specific elements for fidelity are defined, the team sets up a three-column chart for individuals to use. **Column 1:** List the description of the required element, one row for each element. Label this column as Elements **Column 2:** In this column add the question: Comparisons: How is my current practice similar or different from this element? **Column 3:** In this column add the self-assessment question:

Figure 5.6 Conceptual Change Routines

Capacity as Individual Skills and Beliefs

Routine Name: **Presenting New Ideas**	Routine Name: **Systematic Processing**
	I believe with the right supports, I can be successful with this element.
	1 Strongly disagree—
	5 Strongly agree
	3. In a team or whole group meeting use the 3 Column chart and have teachers work through each column.
	4. The school leaders can then collect the individual sheets and analyze for how teachers think about their practice in comparison to the change idea, and their motivation levels.

Figure 5.6 (Cont.)

- What is their overarching orientation for their identity?
- What is their perspective toward knowledge?
- What are their means to attain their values?

Element 2: Self-efficacy

Teachers' self-efficacy is an important belief system for school leaders to develop with individuals. These routines are based on the various information sources from which people develop self-efficacy (Bandura, 1977).

Element 3: Conceptual Change

The Cognitive–Affective Model of Conceptual Change (CAMCC) (Gregoire, 2003) focuses on the idea that when it comes to change, teachers use both cognitive and affective processing when accepting new ideas.

Element 4: Expertise and Deliberate Practice

When first learning something new, it is not very coordinated or easy to do. We spend most of the time in our heads trying to see what we need to be doing. Whether it is swimming, playing the piano, or learning to hold a good class discussion, the first attempts are not that good. Over time, as the performance repeats, we get out of our heads and let things become automatic. This form of learning is a natural phenomenon that helps to save energy and automate things. There is no problem with this state, which is similar to the routine expert. After enough time, people do not need to think about swimming or opening a class session. However, when practice stops at this stage, improvement stops, and over time, these abilities deteriorate (Ericsson and Pool, 2017). This state is called "naïve" practice, which is just doing the same thing repeatedly, expecting your performance to improve (Ericsson and Pool, 2017).

Teachers need to engage in deliberate practice to keep improving. In contrast to following a typical routine and expecting improvement, deliberate practice focuses on:

1. *Setting a clear specific mini goal* in service of a more extensive performance. For instance, if a teacher wants to improve at holding better classroom discussions, he may set an initial goal of giving students a five-minute timeframe to jot their ideas down.
2. *Focusing practice* by setting reminders of the goal and working on it with deliberate intention. From the example above, this teacher could write the goal down in his lesson plans as a visual reminder.
3. *Setting up a feedback system*. People do not improve performance without extensive feedback. Feedback helps narrow the gap between where the skill is and where it could be. It is hard to know if you are improving or having an impact without knowing if what you are doing is right or wrong. For example, this teacher could ask his principal or instructional coach to provide feedback or ask students to provide feedback if their discussion improved. Among others, Hattie discusses feedback as both an essential element of teaching and gathering feedback from students and assessment data to know your impact on learning (Hattie, 2018).
4. *Getting out of the comfort zone*. To get better, people need to get out of their most comfortable routines and move to the edge of their competence. Human performance does not change all at once but needs a constant push for improvement. In the example,

by starting with a focused brainstorming by students and seeing its impact, then adding a triad structure, then using charting to track the discussion, this teacher keeps moving out of his comfort zone to do something he has never done before.

The only way to get better at teaching in this new model of capacity is to deliberately practice aspects of best pedagogy and building a theory of action. In all of these cases, the emphasis moves beyond merely learning about something and embracing the doing and practicing of the skill. I can read about discussions and watch videos, but I will not develop a reliable mental representation and set of enhanced skills until I actually practice in my classroom.

Routine Name: **Defining Expertise**	Routine Name: **Creating a Practice Plan (adapted from** *Expert Practice for Classrooms: Overview* **(2018).**[1]
Uses: Similar to the Coherence Surveys, this routine focuses on how you can help individuals understand what expertise around a new process or practice looks like.	Uses: This routine uses the ideas of deliberate practice to help people create a clear road map of practice and growth. This routine links with the Defining Expertise routine.
Process Steps: 1. After initial training, help others create an Innovation Configuration[1] that describes the process in descriptive terms. (Note: similar to Interpreting Routine.) 2. Clarify variations between levels for what teachers will be doing exactly 3. Over time add clarity for what students will be doing exactly	*Process Steps*: 1. Using the Innovation Configuration created in the Defining Expertise routine, have individuals review the elements of the change idea and descriptions by level. 2. Each individual chooses a specific element and then analyzes the element for specific sub-skill. 3. Each individual then chooses a specific sub-skill that they want to improve.

Figure 5.7 Expertise and Deliberate Practice Routines

Capacity as Individual Skills and Beliefs

Routine Name: **Defining Expertise**	Routine Name: **Creating a Practice Plan** (adapted from *Expert Practice for Classrooms: Overview* (2018).[1]

4. Continue refining the Innovation Configuration until it captures the exact process and can help people determine growth opportunities	4. Each individual writes a clarification plan that describes specific steps or ideas for moving from one level to the next.
	5. Each individual chooses a feedback partner or method to capture feedback on their performance.
	6. The individual practices their sub-skill with deliberate attention and effort.
	7. Have individuals track their practice with criteria such as
	  (a) Understood my goals for practice
	  (b) Practiced in a way that was 100% focused
	  (c) Persisted past frustration in the practice
	  (d) Asked for or collected feedback in some manner
	  (e) Engaged in reflection and planning for next round of practice.
	8. Individuals bring their feedback and reflections together to discuss further support.

[1] Expert Practice for Classrooms: Overview. (2018). Character Lab: University of Pennsylvania

Figure 5.7 (Cont.)

Team Considerations

In sum, the individual level of capacity development is what reformers have focused on through many different reform waves but never really understood what it takes to make all educators adaptive experts. Individual capacity is the level hardest to change and does not react well to policy or structure. This level of capacity includes understanding how experts develop, the role of beliefs and self-efficacy, and how teachers conceptually change toward reform ideas.

As previously discussed, school capacity is a complex adaptive system and develops and emerges through the interaction of this system with other systems at the organizational and team level. After taking the diagnostic, as a team, think more about these systems and consider these questions.

1. Now, how does your school envision capacity? Why does the individual system matter?
2. How do other systems work to support the development of individual expertise and beliefs?
3. Which element of the individual capacity level is most supported by your school? Why?
4. How does your school help support the development of expertise in your teaching staff?
5. How might deliberate practice be used to improve instruction?
6. What are the strongest beliefs among you and your teaching staff? Are those helping or hindering your improvement efforts?
7. How do the beliefs of your teachers compare or contrast with the theories of your change efforts?
8. How might you interpret resistance using the conceptual change model?
9. What are the forms of efficacy information most used in your school? How can you move toward more mastery experiences?
10. How can you get teachers to more systematically process new ideas?

References

Andersen, E. (2019). Learning to learn. *Harvard Business Review*. Winter Special Edition.

Bandura, A. (1977). Self-efficacy: Toward a unifying theory of behavioral change. *Psychological Review,* 84 (2), 191–215.

Bransford, J., Derry, S., Berliner, D. Hammerness, K. and Beckett, K.L (2005). Theories of learning and their roles in teaching. In Darling-Hammond, L. and Bransford, J. (eds) *Preparing teachers for a changing world: What teachers should learn and be able to do.* Jossey Bass.

Chi, M. T.H. (2006). Two approaches to the study of experts' characteristics. In Ericsson, K.A., Charness, N., Feltovich, P.J. and Hoffman, R.R. (eds) *The Cambridge Handbook of Expertise and Expert Performance.* Cambridge University Press.

Erricsson, K.A. (2006). An introduction to the *Cambridge Handbook of Expertise and Expert Performance*: Its development, organization, and content. In Ericsson, K.A., Charness, N., Feltovich, P.J. and Hoffman, R.R. (eds) *The Cambridge Handbook of Expertise and Expert Performance.* Cambridge University Press.

Ericsson, A. and Pool, R. (2017). *Peak: Secrets from the new science of expertise.* First Mariner Books.

Expert Practice for Classrooms: Overview. (2018). Character Lab: University of Pennsylvania.

Fives, H. and Buehl, M. (2008). What do teachers believe? Developing a framework for examining beliefs about teachers' knowledge and ability. *Contemporary Educational Psychology*, 33 (2), 134–176; doi 10.1016/j.cedpsych.2008.01.001

Fives, H. and Buehl, M.M. (2016). Teacher beliefs, in the context of policy reform. *Policy Insights from the Behavioral and Brain Sciences,* 3 (1) 114–121; doi: 10.1177/2372732215623554

Gregoire, M. (2003, June). Is it a challenge or a threat? A dual-process model of teachers cognition and appraisal process during conceptual change. *Educational Psychology Review,* 15 (2), 147–179.

Hattie, J. (2018). *10 Mindframes for visible learning: Teaching for success.* Abingdon: Routledge.

Liou, Y., Canrinus, E.T. and Daly, A.J. (2019). Activating the implementers: The role of organizational expectations, teacher beliefs, and motivation in bringing about reform. *Teaching and Teacher Education,* 79, 60–72.

Markholt, A., Michelson, J. and Fink, S. (2018). *Leading for professional learning: What successful principals do to support teaching practice.* Jossey-Bass.

Rattan, A., Good, C. and Dweck, C. (2012). Its ok—Not everyone can be good at math: Instructors with an entity theory comfort (and demotivate) students. *Journal of Experimental Social Psychology*, 48, 731–737.

Shermer, M. (2011). *The believing brain: From ghosts and gods to politics and conspiracies—How we construct beliefs and restore them as truths.* Times Books.

Tschannen-Moran, M., Wolfolk-Hoy, A. and Hoy, W.K. (1998). Teacher efficacy: Its meaning and measure. *Review of Educational Research,* 68 (202), 202–248.

Tschannen-Moran, M. and Hoy, A. (2001). Teaching efficacy: Capturing an elusive construct. *Teaching and Teacher Education*, 17 (7), 783–805.

Uso-Domenech, J.L. and Nescolarde-Selva, J. (2016). What are belief systems? *Foundations of Science,* 21, 147–152; doi10.1007/s10699-015-9409-z

Wang, H., Hall, N and Rahimi, S. (2015). Self-efficacy and causal attributions in teachers: Effects on burnout, job satisfaction, illness, and quitting intent. *Teaching and Teacher Education*, 47, 120–130; doi 10.1016/j.tate.2014.12.005

Capacity as Effective Teaming

Amanda Lopez seemed lost in thought as she wandered down the hall towards her office after a long day. She had just left a department meeting of the English department at Stonybrook High School. Amanda had made a concerted effort in the past few weeks to attend these meetings believing they were essential venues for teacher learning. Although after her last session, she began to wonder. Reflecting on the English meeting, she saw teachers who wanted the best for their students. Most, though, were unwilling to use this meeting time productively to develop new ideas or resources to use with students. Much of the time was spent in telling war stories of the week and complaining about district policies. Even with a clear agenda that she had required for all team meetings, the department chair quickly went off course. Amanda wondered what had gotten accomplished and why teachers had balked at these meetings.

In contrast, the day before, she had spent an enjoyable hour in the Math department meeting. In this department, the team leader had created a different type of environment. Teachers worked together to tackle common problems of practice in helping students meet the new standards in their state. Students were not seen as problems but as opportunities to dive deeper into how they understand math and the ways teachers could adjust their teaching to meet those needs. Two beginning teachers had been hired in the math department and were provided with extensive support and curriculum guidance during these meetings. As Amanda finally found her way to her office,

Capacity as Effective Teaming

> she wondered how teams at the same schools could be so different in their intent. As she thought about her other departments, she pondered where she could turn. She wanted to make all of her departmental teams into authentic communities of practice, where learning was intentional, new knowledge built, and adults felt affirmed and supported.

Long before Amanda Lopez showed up on the scene, the Stonybrook High School teachers understood the issue. Many of their students' learning challenges were not individual teacher problems, but common problems for their departmental teams that needed collective solutions. Similar to many other industries, teams have become the de facto structure in education for how work gets done. Over time, teams were created at Stonybrook High School to help improve achievement and instruction, yet many were ineffective. Extensive research in schools points to higher performance in schools with higher levels of a professional community, and therefore an essential part of building capacity for learning (Bryk et al., 2010).

Schools are open systems meaning that information and knowledge flow between individuals and teams within the school. Knowledge that forms in teams can transfer to the organization as a whole, locating the team as the prime source of sense-making, learning, and change (see **Figure 6.1** below). As an open system, schools act more like a network

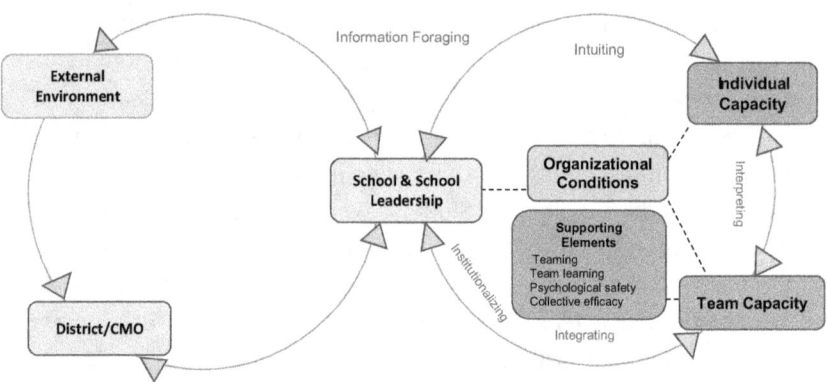

Figure 6.1 Supporting Elements for Team Learning Capacity

in which individuals and teams interact in planned and unplanned ways that eventually lead to how the entire organization learns and functions. However, there is little useful guidance about what it means to learn in a team, how that learning occurs, and why specific teams produce more learning opportunities. As Ms. Lopez saw, in whatever name or form, teams will not provide the necessary structure for learning and problem solving so essential in today's schools without better guidance.

The software analogy fits here again. Teams by themselves are like trying to run a high-powered web-based tool on Windows 95. It just won't work. Instead, school leaders need to know how to create, develop, and maintain high-performing teams based around learning capacity if they are to become more agile and adaptable over time.

This chapter explores a brief history of teams in schools and the necessary concepts leaders need to consider to create learning-focused teams: the nature of teams versus teaming, how learning in teams develops, and the vital role of psychological safety in teams for creating collective efficacy—an offshoot of individual efficacy discussed in Chapter 5. This chapter will also layout specific mindsets, skills, and routines leaders can employ to support high-performing learning teams.

A Brief History of Teams in Education

Much of the writing around teams in schools began in the community of practice research in the sociological and business fields. This conceptual work studied the significance of why teams influenced an organization and its bottom line. Communities of practice define as "groups of people sharing concerns, problems, or a passion for a topic, and who deepen their knowledge and expertise in this area by interacting on an ongoing basis" (Wegner et al., 2002). Over time, these groups develop an approach, a perspective on their work, and a collective body of knowledge, tools, and practices.

In one sense, these communities develop a way of interacting as a social group that can influence individual learning (Wegner, 2002). Much of the emphasis around communities of practice is that these teams are a practical and efficient way to create, manage, and share new knowledge. Communities of practice, though, do not see knowledge as mere facts. Instead, understanding develops as the "accumulation of experience—a kind of residue of their actions, thinking, and conversations—that remains a dynamic part of their ongoing experience" (Wegner et al., 2002). This accumulation of experience is the tacit knowledge that is hard to develop and capture in more traditional learning formats and requires social interaction among people. Because knowledge is dynamic and the environment in which we operate is so volatile, how we innovate, experiment, and learn requires different learning structures.

In the field of education, previous decades of research used the term professional communities of practice to describe the potential power of schools that use teams. Early research on professional communities in school pointed to the potential power of an active professional community. This work found that collegiality in high-performing schools went beyond supportive relationships. These schools demonstrated a professional community that exhibited norms of innovation and learning around ways to help all students succeed. These communities were focused on student learning and improving instructional practices together.

However, like many others in the educational space, this potential failed to take hold widespread due to a lack of knowledge, will, and institutional beliefs and patterns. A lack of coordination and team development efforts often hindered teams' work in the late 1990s and early 2000s, limiting the impact of this robust structure.

Professional Learning Communities

The evolution of Professional Learning Communities (PLC's) has been the most significant attempt to address many previous problems with professional communities. The assumption of PLCs suggests that if a school uses this structure, teachers will increase their professional knowledge, which will improve student learning. Some studies show this may be true (Vescio et al., 2008).

In a 2008 meta-analysis, Vescio et al. found that "In a general sense, all 11 research articles used in this analysis supported the idea that participation in a learning community leads to changes in teaching practice." And that, "All eight studies that examined the relationship between teachers' participation in PLCs and student achievement found that student learning improved." However, there was no clear indication from these studies how this learning improved.

Other studies suggest that the problem of understanding the impact of PLCs has to do with a lack of conceptual clarity. Because of too many conceptual anchors and not understanding how they influence teachers and students, PLCs are hard to define. In essence, differing visions and concepts surround the notion of a PLC, making it sometimes challenging to implement and use correctly. In their meta-analysis, Lomos et al. (2011) found different but positive results in student achievement. These authors suggest that for PLCs to have a more substantial impact, clearer conceptualizations of essential elements and purposes need establishing (Lomos et al., 2011). Like previous studies, there was no clear indication of why and how this structural reform influences teachers' learning or transfers to their practice.

Researchers have also looked at schools as workplaces. Schools are "learning environments that are negotiated and constructed by individuals ... as well as the cultural norms and practices being exercised through the work practice" (Billett, 2004). From this perspective, researchers found that 83% of teachers in this study experienced tensions around workplace pressure, interpersonal tensions, and shared learning processes. Learning processes included the need for collaborative and agentic learning within competing visions for learning (Schaap et al., 2018).

In sum, over the past decade, the advent of Professional Learning Communities has increased due to pressures about raising student achievement. The preliminary evidence for increasing student achievement through this structure shows promise. However, the overarching purpose for PLCs in some venues is still not understood, nor are the specific ways to improve the learning and practice of teachers within PLCs.

Some suggest that PLCs continue to struggle and take hold due to the "deep rules" of collaboration. Sutton and House (2019) state:

> "Like any other social group people find themselves in, PLCs are ruled by tacit norms, routines, and procedures that are deeply social and cultural in nature and that are many times specific both to the teaching profession and to the specific characteristics of a school." Protocols are often used to help with the structuring of PLC's. However, protocols do little to penetrate the "deep rules" that exist between novice and experienced, male and female, high status, and low-status teachers.

Evidence for PLC's shows they are promising, but with these issues in mind, how can we ensure learning occurs? Some recent research has argued the need for more collaborative professionalism that articulates how members of a profession work together "rather than only talk, share, and reflect together" (Hargreaves and O'Connor, 2018). We turn to one promising way next.

Effective Teaming

To help many PLC's meet their original intent of learning, we need to reestablish the verb form of teams into teaming. Teaming as a set of processes, routines, and beliefs is "essential to an organization's ability to respond to opportunities …" (Edmondson, 2012). People in schools need to learn together if many of the problems of complexity are to be solved. Many theorists regard collective learning in teams as the primary avenue for learning at the organizational level (Edmondson, 2012).

Teaming in the verb form is not merely about the structural element. Instead, teaming is the deliberate activity of working and learning together, no matter if the designated team is short-lived or longer-term in nature. According to Edmondson (2012), "Teaming blends relating to people, listening to other viewpoints, coordinating actions, and making shared decisions. Effective teaming requires everyone to remain vigilantly aware of others' needs, roles, and perspectives." Effective teaming also organizes around the primary purpose of informal and formal learning that can influence a teacher's practice over time.

Edmondson (2012) goes on to describe teaming as "largely determined by the mindset and practices of teamwork, not by the design and structures of effective teams. Teaming is teamwork on the fly." Most teams in education execute strategy from the top. For example, in the PLC movement, the strategy of benchmark assessments is followed whether students are ready or not. This routine or structure primarily follows organizing to execute.

In contrast, teams that organize to learn use teaming as a verb to generate ideas, find solutions to student learning issues, and learn from each other about effective pedagogical moves. Similar to teams in the modern workplace, teaming for learning, "involves what's called reciprocal interdependence, where back-and-forth communication and coordination are essential to getting work done" (Edmondson, 2012, 2018). The notion of teaming as organizing to learn asks that teams plan, take action, and reflect on that action to modify that action if needed. Again Edmondson (2012, 2018) suggests:

> Collective learning includes such activities as collecting, sharing, or analyzing information; obtaining and reflecting on feedback from customers or others; and active experimentation. Individual learning behaviors within a collective learning experience include the following:
>
> - Asking questions
> - Sharing information
> - Seeking help
> - Experimenting with unproven actions
> - Talking about mistakes
> - Seeking feedback

Using teaming for the learning needs a clear focus for that learning. Since teaching is ultimately a profoundly complex process, process knowledge needs to be a clear focus for team learning. Process knowledge is a crucial term meaning knowledge about how to produce the desired result. This knowledge, of course, differs by discipline, age, outcome, and many other factors. This process knowledge also varies by the "maturity of the cause and effect relationships" (Edmondson et al., 2007).

In situations when uncertainty is low, like classroom management, routine knowledge suffices and can easily be shared. In contrast, in other cases where we may have little experience on how to achieve results, innovation and experimentation are needed along with ongoing deliberation and sharing of results. For example, teaching all students to higher standards or different non-academic outcomes requires teaming for learning since the knowledge base has not been completely established.

To summarize, previous work on professional learning communities focused on the what-the structural element- without a clear understanding of the process or purpose of teams. In essence, we have focused on the noun form of teams without a clear focus on why they are necessary and how they should perform: the verb form. This is explored below.

Learning in Teams

> As Amanda Lopez joined her math team's work over the next few weeks, she noticed they operated much differently than teams she had watched in the past. While they often talked about the curriculum and pacing of their courses, her math team was also cognizant that unfinished learning resulted from common pacing leaving many students behind, especially in Algebra I courses. Because of this theory, the team had started to create a plan of small inquiry cycles to help students finish their learning and collect data and information about their actions. Each meeting was used not only to look at data but also to learn from it to inform the next actions.

The advent of PLCs has been a way for educators to use a new structure to assist in student achievement. A more in-depth question asks, "Are PLCs avenues for teacher and organizational learning, are they tools that help maintain consistency and predictability, or are they some sort of internally inconsistent combination of both" (Van Lare and Brazer, 2013)? As we have argued, learning at the individual and team level is a requirement for learning at the organizational level. Thus, the need to know if and how learning is occurring is central to building capacity at the team level. As Van Lare and Brazeer (2013) stated:

> We argue that weaknesses exist in the current theory base for empirical work on PLCs. First, little empirical research is rooted in established learning theory... the creation and development of PLCs runs the risk of neglecting the movement's central purpose: teacher learning ...

Most of the work done around the implementation of PLCs has argued for the fidelity within the principles of PLC structure without attending to one of the primary applications of a PLC: teacher learning. Team effectiveness is not the same as effectiveness in teacher learning. Contextual factors, personality and belief factors, and other influences account for how teacher learning is affected. Most models of PLC's or professional communities proposed to date do not identify learning processes within teacher communities or the interactions between teams and the extended organization (Van Lare and Brazeer, 2013; Seidel-Horn and Kane, 2015).

PLC's by recipe, therefore, become a danger to true collaboration and learning. PLC's can constrict efforts to enhance learning "because of a limited examination of how teachers learn, how their learning might be connected to change, and the influence of organizational context" (Van Lare and Brazeer, 2013).

To better understand learning and opportunities to learn within teams, Seidel-Horn and Kane (2015) studied various teams across various schools. She wanted to understand more in-depth the assumptions surrounding teacher teams and improved student performance. By analyzing what teachers talked about and what they said in their teams, they found that not all teams have the same generativity level for teacher learning. She posited that

> the capacity for deep collaboration among teachers remains questionable. ... Given the paucity of mere idea sharing among teachers in the recent past—an activity that does not approach the complexity of collaborative pedagogical problem solving (Seidel-Horn, 2010)—typical school cultures may not yet be ripe for the kind of collaboration that supports transformative learning.
> (Seidel-Horn and Kane, 2015)

As a sociocultural system, team conversations operate as a collective zone of proximal development (ZPD) for teachers that allow them to see what may be possible with their students (Seidel-Horn and Kane, 2015). Hall and Seidel-Horn's (2012) research shows that three conceptual resources shape teachers' opportunities to learn.

1. *Representational practices* are how people can build a collective understanding of their pedagogy and interpret classroom situations and learning. These practices build upon artifacts like samples of student work. Or they can use methods such as when a team uses a *Replay* to recall past instructional interactions or *Rehearsals* which anticipate future instructional interactions. For example, a team of teachers produces a lesson together and rehearses what they will say to introduce the lesson.
2. *Problem framing* describes how teachers define various issues. In teaching teams, frames work in multiple ways. They can

organize collective attention or shift the meaning of activities. Frames can also position teachers to varying degrees as agents in the problems they face, which all influence the opportunity to learn from conversations. For example, instead of seeing a lack of engagement as only a student issue, a team of teachers looks at how their approach to a unit could hinder engagement.

3. An *epistemic stance* describes the position teachers take on what can be known; how to know it; and why it matters for teaching and learning. "Whether at the level of activity or utterance, epistemic stances are conveyed, negotiated, and reinstated through the language teachers use to communicate about their work. Language is thus a means both for representing and for understanding problems of practice" (Hall and Seidel-Horn, 2012). For example, in math, a team of teachers moves toward having students make sense of why a procedure works instead of merely repeating the procedure.

Recall that, from a situated learning perspective, people learn from the socially cultural perspectives of the community. Different representational practices, problem framing, and epistemic stances will lead to vast differences in how teams learn from one another. By using these three conceptual resources, leaders can support teams for better learning.

When comparing across various teams, Seidel-Horn and Little (2010) found, for example:

- As instruction became more ambitious, time spent on defining problems of practice increased.
- The conceptual resource used most frequently across all teams were epistemic claims and representations of practice. How various teams used these resources though were qualitatively different. More sophisticated groups included students and student thinking with higher frequency. More accomplished teachers in these groups considered student experience and perspectives more frequently, which helped shape the thinking of others.
- In math groups, more sophisticated groups used epistemic claims that reflected math learning as sense-making and integrated thinking around teaching, students, and math more frequently. These groups

also linked epistemic claims and representations of practice more regularly. They also used more robust and complex epistemic claims than other groups.

In sum, across numerous studies, groups, and schools, this research points out that more sophisticated groups focus primarily on instructional problems. There were substantial overlaps in their use of these conceptual resources that characterized their talk allowing for more profound influence and learning among members of the group. These teachers and groups placed student thinking at the center of their sense-making about teaching. By emphasizing students' affective and intellectual experiences with mathematics instruction, the teachers designed ways that were more instructionally specific (Seidel-Horn and Little, 2010).

The Role of Psychological Safety in Teaming

> As Ms. Lopez continued to analyze her different teams, she began to uncover how people treated each other and responded to one another in team meetings. When she sat in the English meetings, she felt a sense of anxiety as teachers continually jabbed at each other and often made fun of students and other teachers in the building. When teachers tried to raise concerns, they were often laughed at or criticized, reducing people's willingness to speak up. In contrast, the math department had a much different feel to it. Teachers were highly supportive of one another and showed vulnerability in bringing up issues around their teaching, knowing they would receive numerous suggestions. Ms. Lopez continued to wonder what the real differences were and how she could foster a more supportive and learning-focused feeling across all of her teams.

You have probably heard of the now-famous Google study done on teams. If you haven't, here is a short recap. Like many big tech industries, Google has moved to teams and networks of teams to get most of their essential work accomplished. To develop more effective teams, the HR department at Google decided to study what makes the most effective teams. Their initial working hypothesis was that great teams had great leaders with just the right people. According to them:

> We were dead wrong. Who is on a team matters less than how the team members interact, structure their work, and view their contributions. So much for that magical algorithm.
>
> We learned that five key dynamics set successful teams apart from other teams at Google:

1. Psychological safety: Can we take risks on this team without feeling insecure or embarrassed?
2. Dependability: Can we count on each other to do high-quality work on time?
3. Structure & clarity: Are goals, roles, and execution plans on our team clear?
4. Meaning of work: Are we working on something personally important for each of us?
5. Impact of work: Do we fundamentally believe that the work we're doing matters?

The interactions of the Google teams around dependability, clarity, meaning, and impact are similar to research done on PLC's. However, the idea of psychological safety as the foundation for effective teams has not appeared in any educational research on teams, professional communities, or PLCs to date. In Google's research, psychological safety was the most critical dynamic at play in any team studied. So, what is psychological safety, and why is the most essential condition on a team?

Edmondson's research has also studied the dynamics of psychological safety in much of her research. In the *Fearless Organization* (2019), Edmondson lays out the premise that because we are in a knowledge-based society, the sharing of new knowledge from experience is a critical part of any organization's success. "For knowledge work to flourish, the workplace must be one where people feel able to share their knowledge" (Edmondson, 2019). This sharing usually occurs in teams because this structure is more flexible and agile than the organization. These teams are typically dynamic and ever-shifting based on need.

Sharing, however, always runs up against interpersonal fears. People have a fear of looking foolish or showing they are not as smart as others on the team. Or in the worst case, fearing for their jobs if they say something wrong. Safe is better than sorry and avoids social rejection. In essence, social belonging is innate in us as humans. We do not want others to think less of us, so we often hide what we know or what we want to learn to be successful (Edmondson, 2019). We don't want to stand out or look dumb, and we don't want to ruin work relationships.

Edmondson's (2019) findings suggest that psychological safety lives at the group level and defines it as "a climate in which people are comfortable expressing and being themselves," or "the belief that the work environment is safe for interpersonal risk-taking." On a more concrete level, psychological safety also represents "a belief that one will not be punished or humiliated for speaking up with ideas, questions, or concerns, or mistakes, and that the team is safe for interpersonal risk-taking" (Edmondson, 1999).

Many of us have been part of an organization or team in which questing or speaking up, while not clearly forbidden, was dismissed at the first sign of tension. When all teams develop this sense of psychological safety, a fearless organization emerges. Edmondson (2019) states, "interpersonal fear is minimized so that team and organizational performance can be maximized in a knowledge-intensive world." When people feel fear and don't share or speak up, innovation and growth recede. Without psychological safety, learning at the team and organizational level is almost sure not to occur. Cultures of silence can become dangerous cultures.

In sum, research at the group level has shown psychological safety and trust can be built. Once built, psychological safety leads to information sharing and decreasing conflict frequency, leading to improved learning and performance. This psychological safety rests on an active context for sharing, team leadership, problem-solving, task conflict skills, social interaction, and diversity of opinions. Eventually, this psychological safety can lead to enhanced collective efficacy.

The Role of Collective Efficacy

To help her get a better sense of how each department member viewed their team and how it was working, Ms. Lopez had been interviewing all the teachers on the English and Math teams. Now, as

> she was reviewing her notes, Ms. Lopez saw that the English teachers did not have a lot of respect for specific teachers on their team. One teacher stated it bluntly when she said, " I have no idea what is being taught in the course before mine and I frequently have to reteach a lot of what they say they are teaching. When I ask, people get very defensive. It is a disaster." In contrast, one of her veteran math teachers suggested, " I know exactly what is being taught in the courses before mine and how it is being taught. If students come in with holes, I feel I can talk to everybody about it, and we can fix it on the spot."

So far, we have looked at teaming versus teams, learning in teams, and the role of psychological safety to enable more adult learning to occur. One final element of team capacity is the role of collective efficacy. In his seminal work on the ideas and strategies that most impact student achievement, Hattie (2018) found collective efficacy as having the highest effect size or relation to student learning. Just like individual efficacy, teams that develop collective efficacy as both an outcome of their work and as an enabling resource have a more significant impact on student learning (Goddard et al., 2004).

Bandura (1997) originally defined collective efficacy as a "group's shared belief in its conjoint capabilities to organize and execute courses of action required to produce given levels of attainment." This definition was simplified for schools and "refers to the perceptions of teachers in a school that the faculty as a whole can organize and execute the courses of action required to have a positive effect on students" (Goddard, 2004).

Teams that are characterized by high levels of collective efficacy see problems or setbacks not as obstacles but as challenges to be met and overcome. These teams exhibit "creativity, resiliency, and commitment required to reach performance goals" (Goddard and Salloum, 2011). Collective efficacy is an emergent characteristic of schools and teams, which gains its meaning from collective perceptions (Hoy et al., 2002).

Self-efficacy shows that an individual's choices and agency rest on their perception that they will do well on a task. Similarly, collective efficacy is based on beliefs about a team or faculty's ability to impact students' achievement. Teachers with high self-efficacy have been shown to use various techniques to set norms of expectation and impact student learning. Similarly, teams or schools with high levels of collective efficacy "serve to influence the behavior of individuals and the normative environment of collectives by providing expectations about the likelihood of success for various pursuits" (Goddard and Goddard, 2001).

In essence, the shared beliefs and expectations of success from the team influence the individual's beliefs and actions to meet those expectations. The team acts with a collective agency or the intentional pursuit of a course of action. "Strong collective efficacy leads teachers to be more persistent in their teaching efforts, set high and reasonable goals, and overcome temporary setbacks and failures" (Hoy et al., 2002). Teams exercise collective agency on each other even if they don't know it. When it comes to collective efficacy, the question to ask is, "can we orchestrate the thoughts and actions necessary to perform the task successfully" (Goddard and Salloum, 2011).

Collective efficacy has been studied across many types of organizations and many human fields, including neighborhood health, neighborhood violence, athletic teams, nursing teams, and different manufacturing industries. In all of these various studies, one notable finding sticks out. No matter the group or group goal studied, "collective efficacy beliefs have consistently predicted group success on diverse measures of attainment" (Goddard and Salloum, 2011).

The same finding exists for schools. For instance, Bandura (1993) in the first study of collective efficacy and student achievement, found that student achievement at the school level correlated highly with collective efficacy. He also found that collective efficacy had a greater effect on student achievement than did student SES (Bandura, 1993). A similar study looked at the relationship between teacher efficacy and collective efficacy. Findings showed that a one standard deviation increase in collective efficacy was associated with a 0.248 standard deviation increase in teacher efficacy—again showing the link between the collective and individuals (Goddard and Goddard, 2001).

Last, a study looked at the relationship between academic press, collective efficacy, and math achievement in high schools. The authors found that collective efficacy had a strong correlation with math achievement and had the highest independent effect on achievement (Hoy et al., 2002).

In sum, as the authors of the last study state: "We were successful in finding a variable, collective efficacy, that was more important in explaining school achievement than SES. This latter finding is of practical significance because it is easier to change the collective efficacy of a school than it is to influence the SES of the school" (Hoy et al., 2002).

Diagnosing Team Learning Elements

Just like the previous chapter when we explored the interaction of individual learning with other parts of our model, we again take a systems perspective. This perspective allows you to see how various systems and their elements interact in a mutually supportive manner. For example, in team learning, we hypothesize that effective teaming skills lead to enhanced psychological safety and team learning skills. These learning skills, in turn, lead to greater collective efficacy on the team.

If we use the teaming and collective efficacy research together, we also surmise that the creation of effective teams will impact individual learning. For instance, we discussed above that the collective efficacy of a team influences individual efficacy. Growth in individual efficacy can then change individual beliefs and help develop personal expertise. Similarly, teams with a high degree of psychological safety will promote personalized learning around the organizational conditions of clarity of purpose and instructional guidance.

As you can see in our proposed model (see **Figure 6.1**), teams sit in the middle between individual and organizational learning and help develop both systems. To get a general sense of the status of these elements that support team learning in your school, take a few minutes, and consider the following diagnostic individually or as a team.

Leading to Create Team Learning Capacity

> Amanda Lopez realized that most of her staff sat on teams but were not very advanced yet in their teaming, creating psychological safety, learning as a team, or creating collective efficacy. She again recognized that from a distributed perspective, she could not work with every team, but would need to develop her leadership team to develop the teams they led. The focus on teaming, psychological safety, team learning, and collective efficacy would need deliberate practice and attention to develop team learning capacity.

Capacity as Effective Teaming

Team Learning Level: The school develops the necessary elements and routines to support ongoing team learning about external demands and areas for internal improvement.

Processes and supports at this level of learning	Diagnostic questions	Responses 1. Highly inaccurate 2. Somewhat inaccurate 3. Not sure 4. Somewhat accurate 5. Highly accurate
1. Teaming	1a. At our school, we use both short-term and long-term teams for much of our work.	1 2 3 4 5
	1b. At our school, our teams spend time on the affective dimensions of working together.	1 2 3 4 5
	1c. At our school, our teams typically collect, share, and analyze information together.	1 2 3 4 5
	1d. At our school, our teams are responsive to the needs of all of our students.	1 2 3 4 5 Total ____/4=
2. Learning in Teams	2a. In our team(s) we use processes for collective inquiry around common problems of practice.	1 2 3 4 5
	2b. In our team(s) we use joint work to learn from our actions.	1 2 3 4 5
	2c. In our team(s) we believe that we are interdependent.	1 2 3 4 5
	2d. In our team(s), we use representation practices (collective lesson planning, student work, replaying and rehearsal, etc.)	1 2 3 4 5

Figure 6.2 Team Learning Diagnostic

Capacity as Effective Teaming

Processes and supports at this level of learning	Diagnostic questions	Responses
	2e. In our team(s) we frame learning problems around both teaching and learning issues.	1 2 3 4 5
	2f. In our team(s) we believe we can learn collectively from our actions.	1 2 3 4 5
	2g. In our team(s) we take time to learn from our failures.	1 2 3 4 5
		Total ____/7=
3. Psychological safety	3a. People on my team are eager to share information about what does and does not work.	1 2 3 4 5
	3b. Making mistakes is considered part of the learning process on our teams.	1 2 3 4 5
	3c. If I make a mistake on my team, it will not be held against me.	1 2 3 4 5
	3d. On my team, teaches feel comfortable experimenting with untried teaching approaches, even if the approach might not work.	1 2 3 4 5
	3e. On my team, it is easy to speak up about what is on your mind.	1 2 3 4 5
	3f. People on my team are usually comfortable talking about problems and disagreements about teaching and learning.	1 2 3 4 5
		Total ____/6=

Figure 6.2 (Cont.)

Processes and supports at this level of learning	Diagnostic questions	Responses
4. Collective Efficacy	4a. Teachers on my team are confident they will be able to motivate their students.	1 2 3 4 5
	4b. Teachers on my team have the skills needed to produce meaningful student learning.	1 2 3 4 5
	4c. If a child doesn't learn something, teachers on my team will try another way.	1 2 3 4 5
	4d. Teachers on my team believe that every child can learn.	1 2 3 4 5
	4e. Teachers on my team are skilled in various methods of teaching.	1 2 3 4 5
	4f. On my team, teachers have what it takes to explore new instructional approaches to help underperforming students.	1 2 3 4 5
		Total ____/6=

Figure 6.2 (Cont.)

Capacity Model Area	Leadership Mindsets	Leadership Skills
3. **Interpreting** (individual and team learning)	• Crafting meaning • Growth mindset	1. Developing and analyzing teaming and using learning processes 2. Creating psychological safety 3. Influencing collective efficacy 4. Building short inquiry cycles and narrowing to action 5. Developing team processing

Figure 6.3 Leadership Mindsets and Skills for Team Learning

Leadership Mindsets and Skills

To help create team learning capacity, all leaders of teams will need to develop two new mindsets. First, leaders will need to become skillful at helping team members make or craft meaning from their team learning opportunities as they begin to take on and interpret new ideas or new techniques for solving issues of learning. Second, a growth mindset will also be essential as leaders work with teams to develop psychological safety and learn from failure. Leadership skills to develop these conditions are listed below and emanate from these two mindsets.

Routines for Team Learning Capacity

In sum, teams are an important work structure for any organization, including schools. Because of their importance, leaders need to help support teams, focus them on learning, and help foster psychological safety to help create collective efficacy. The routines described below are ways that the capacity of team skills and beliefs can develop.

These routines for the team system require school leaders to understand how teams best develop, how psychological safety develops, and how that leads to collective efficacy over time. By creating and using these routines, teaming can be enacted and developed to support learning at the team level (see **Figure 6.4** below for a list of these routines).

Routine Name: **Developing Psychological Safety with Check-ins**	Routine Name: **Ways of Working (Adapted from Jarrell, 2017)**

Uses: This routine can be used to help develop the risk-taking vulnerability associated with developing psychological safety on a team.
 	
Process Steps:
1. At the start of each team meeting, each member is asked to check in.
2. Various questions can be used but should focus on:
  (a) Current emotional state
  (b) A risk or challenge that was taken this past week
3. Each check in should be between 30–60 seconds
4. Team leader summarizes
	Uses: This routine can be used to develop ways of working together to begin a school year or when new teams are formed.
	
	Process Steps:
	1. A team leader has teams members list ways their values and beliefs around teams and working together.
	2. Next, the team leader begins to chart out how the team responds to the following: How will we behave based on those values:
	  (a) Communicate—When, how, and with what channels?
	  (b) Collaborate—When will we show each other our work? How will we work together on new ideas? What tools will we use?
	  (c) Safety—How can we take safe risks on this team? How can we surface and learn from mistakes?
	  (d) Measure our work—What does success look like? How will we know we've reached it?
	  (e) Feedback—How do we expect feedback will be delivered and managed/
	  (f) Decisions—Is it through consensus or is there a designated decision-maker? How will decisions be communicated? What happens if we get stuck?

Figure 6.4 Teaming for Learning Routines

Routine Name: **Developing Psychological Safety with Check-ins**	Routine Name: **Ways of Working (Adapted from Jarrell, 2017)**
	(g) Recognition—How do we individually like to be recognized and rewarded? Do we have specific goals and milestones we'll celebrate together? (h) Conflict—What does healthy conflict look like for us? What would unhealthy conflict look like? (i) Priorities—How do we prioritize the work? How will we resolve conflicting priorities? (j) Archetype—What is our symbol? Our spirit animal, superhero, or historical figure? Why? 3. From these responses, the leader then begins the process of narrowing these ideas down into commitments and expectations asking: How will we show up differently as a member of this team? What behavior changes can we hold each other to?

Routine Name: **Kicking off the Learning Cycle**	Routine Name: **Rehearsals and Replays**
Uses: This routine can be used any time a team starts a new learning cycle or project.	*Uses*: This routine can help people build a collective understanding of their pedagogy and situations that happened during teaching.

Figure 6.4 (Cont.)

Capacity as Effective Teaming

Routine Name: **Kicking off the Learning Cycle**	Routine Name: **Rehearsals and Replays**
Process Steps:	*Process Steps*:
1. Team leaders sets the stage and reminds team of their focus on learning	1. After creating a lesson, teachers discuss what section may be most challenging.
2. Develop individual purpose statements using a simple stem: Our purpose for this learning cycle is to _____.	2. With that part, teachers discuss how to phrase that part for clarity, support struggling students, or best examples to use.
3. Consolidate the purpose statements into one.	3. Teachers then practice or rehearse that section.
4. Discuss and add specific drivers for why the team is pursuing this learning project.	4. Teachers discuss work samples or responses they want to gather to analyze.
5. Discuss the project scope (e.g. what's in and out of scope).	5. After using that section in class, teachers regather and replay the section.
6. Create a rough timeline by drawing a line starting with today and ending at some end point. Add estimated milestones along the line.	6. Student responses or work samples are analyzed to see how the design of that section impacted student learning.
7. Design the architecture for the learning project (might include new lessons, new structures, new processes etc.).	7. Team leader works to distill patterns of responses.
8. Have people write down what they think will make the project a success and list out.	8. Teachers discuss necessary adjustments.
9. Work through the following: (a) Risks—Things that could affect quality or timing (b) Assumptions—Current truths that if changed could create an issue (c) Issues—Things that have already adversely affected the project	

Figure 6.4 (Cont.)

Routine Name: **Kicking off the Learning Cycle**	Routine Name: **Rehearsals and Replays**
(d) Dependencies—Things that need to be done regularly to make project a success 10. Create a communication or check in schedule	

Routine Name: **Pulling Knowledge (Adapted from Leonard, 2005)**	Routine Name: **After Action Reviews or Learning from Failure**
Uses: To learn from an expert with extensive tacit knowledge. This process can last any length of time.	*Uses*: After a degree of psychological safety is created on a team, collective trials and experiments can be run. After a trial is run, this protocol can be used to determine why it may not have been as successful as it could have been.
Process Steps: 1. Determine who you will acquire knowledge from 2. Follow the OPPTY process: • Observation • Practice • Partnering • Joint problem solving • Take responsibility 3. Use action plans and learning logs focused on insights to track learning.	*Process Steps*: 1. The team lead creates a two-column chart with one side labeled students and the other side labeled teachers with Potential Causes of Failure listed on the side. 2. The team reviews the Potential Causes of Failure discussed in Chapter 6. 3. For the student side, each team member is given three votes on what they believe caused the failure with supporting rationale. 4. Team discusses reasons and comes to a consensus on 1–2 primary causes of failure. 5. For the teacher side, each team member is given three votes on what they believe caused the failure with supporting rationale.

Figure 6.4 (Cont.)

Routine Name: **Pulling Knowledge** (Adapted from Leonard, 2005)	Routine Name: **After Action Reviews or Learning from Failure**
	6. Team discusses reasons and comes to a consensus on 1–2 primary causes of failure. 7. Team brainstorms on ways to overcome the failure and develops their next learning cycle.

Routine Name: **Project Health Monitor**	Routine Name: **Team Health Monitor**
Uses: This routine is a way to have each team monitor their actions and performance against the attributes that lead to successful projects.	*Uses*: This routine is a way to have each team monitor their performance against the attributes that overall lead to successful teams. A school leader can also use this list to observe teams and offer feedback or coaching.

Process Steps:
1. Team leader reviews need for ongoing analysis of team functioning.
2. After reading the attribute out loud, all team members will vote on a count of three.
  (a) Thumbs up- "we're strong here"
  (b) Thumbs sideways—"we're ok— but could improve"
  (c) Thumbs down—"we're struggling here and need to improve"
3. Read the attributes out loud. These can include the following or develop your own.
  (a) There is someone who is leading the project.
  (b) Roles and responsibilities are clear and agreed upon.
	Process Steps:
	1. Team leader reviews need for ongoing analysis of team functioning.
	2. After reading the attribute out loud, all team members will vote on a count of three.
	  (a) Thumbs up—"we're strong here"
	  (b) Thumbs sideways— "we're ok— but could improve"
	  (c) Thumbs down—"we're struggling here and need to improve"
	3. Read the attributes out loud. These can include the following or develop your own. (Note only focus on 1–2 per meeting.)

Figure 6.4 (Cont.)

Capacity as Effective Teaming

Routine Name: **Project Health Monitor**	Routine Name: **Team Health Monitor**
(c) The team has a common purpose and understand why they are here. (d) It's clear what success means—it is defined, with a clear goal, and how it will be measured. (e) Some sort of need for this project or change ideas has been established. (f) The plan has been summarized, written down, and shared with the team. (g) Clear understanding of dependencies (h) Team is making progress by following timelines, learning along the way, and using lessons learned. (i) Gathering insights 4. Team reviews ratings and discusses lowest areas with next steps or actions to improve.	**(a) Psychological safety** 1 Mistakes are accepted on this team 2 Members of this team are able to bring up problems and tough issues. 3 People on this team sometimes accept others for being different. 4 It is safe to take a risk on this team. 5 It is easy to ask other members of this team for help. 6 No one on this team would deliberately act in a way that undermines my efforts. 7 Working with members of this team, my unique skills and talents are valued and utilized. **(b) Dependability** 1. I feel we have a mutual obligation for one another to succeed 2. I know I can depend on my teammates for help 3. Relationships are strong on this team 4. My teammates have my back. **(c) Structures and clarity** 1. We frequently collect, share and analyze information and data 2. We experiment and innovate with unproven actions through joint action 3. We often initiate our own ideas and seek feedback from one another 4. We always determine a clear purpose for projects or new ideas **(d) Meaning** 1. I am really enthusiastic about the mission of my school

Figure 6.4 (Cont.)

Routine Name: **Project Health Monitor**	Routine Name: **Team Health Monitor**
	2. In my work, I am always challenged to grow. 3. Most of our work together ends up with some lessons I can learn from. **(e) Impact** 1. Our team has organized primarily to learn together. 2. We talk about and learn from our mistakes 3. We believe most problems can be solved if we study it in-depth together
Routine Name: **Creating Collective-Efficacy**	Routine Name: **Changing Your Inner Narrative (Adapted from Andersen, 2019)**
Uses: This routine uses the sources of information from which teachers develop self-efficacy to help the team develop a sense of accomplishment. This routine can be done with teams, and can be used on an ongong basis to open or close conversations to help create more collective efficacy.	*Uses*: To help build team efficacy, build team-awareness, and focus on growth opportunities. This simple routine can be used in group situations.
Process Steps: 1. A team leader or administrator opens with a review of the change happening and why it is important to reflect and review successes. 2. Have individuals reflect on and list successes their team has had with new change ideas and their impact on students.	*Process Steps*: 1. Explain that our self-talk and group talk is often what inhibits our abilities to make meaningful progress in our practice. 2. Give examples of unsupportive self-talk • We don't need to learn this • We are already fine at this • This is boring • We are terrible at this

Figure 6.4 (Cont.)

Capacity as Effective Teaming

Routine Name: **Creating Collective-Efficacy**	Routine Name: **Changing Your Inner Narrative (Adapted from Andersen, 2019)**
3. Have individuals share their accomplishments (note this step is using the information source as performance accomplishments as well as hearing others' accomplishments can lead to vicarious experiences—another information source). 4. The team leader or administrator then describes successes they have seen (again using vicarious experience information sources). 5. Last the team leader or administrator discusses positive effort of individuals and how they are handling the changes (again using verbal persuasion and emotional arousal as information sources)	3. Ask these more supportive questions and have individuals write down their responses • What would our team's future look like if we did learn this? • Are we really fine at this? How do we compare with others? • I wonder why others find it interesting. • We are making beginner mistakes, but we'll get better. 4. Have the team reflect on their responses and how pre and post responses can help develop a growth mindset.

Figure 6.4 (Cont.)

Team Considerations

1. Now, how does your school envision capacity? Why does the team learning matter?
2. How do other levels of learning work to support the development of effective teaming?
3. How does teaming work to support different learning levels in your school?
4. How do your teams work to support the learning of each other?
5. Is the role of learning explicit on your teams, or do they exist to help manage?
6. Which of your teams have high degrees of psychological safety? Why?
7. Which of your teams struggle with psychological safety? Why?

8. How do you know if a team has psychological safety?
9. What do you look for to know if your teams have a learning purpose?
10. How do you know if your teams have collective efficacy? How can you help build collective efficacy through the four sources of efficacy information?

References

Andersen, E. (2019). Learning to learn. *Harvard Business Review,* Winter Special Edition.

Bandura, A. (1993). Perceived self-efficacy in cognitive development and functioning. *Educational Psychologist*, 28, 117–148.

Bandura, A. (1997). *Self-efficacy: The exercise of control.* Freeman.

Billett, S. (2004). Workplace participatory practices: conceptualising workplaces as learning environment. *Journal of Workplace Learning,* 16, 312–324; doi:10.1108/13665620410550295

Bryk, A.S., Sebring, P.B., Allensworth, E., Luppescu, S. and Easton, J.Q. (2010). *Organizing schools for improvement: Lessons from Chicago.* University of Chicago Press.

Catalina L, Hofman, R.H. and Bosker, R.J (2011). Professional communities and student achievement – a meta-analysis. *School Effectiveness and School Improvement*, 22 (2), 121–148.

Edmondson, A. (1999). Psychological safety and learning behavior in work teams. *Administrative Science Quarterly*, 44 (2), 350–383.

Edmondson, A. (2012). *Teaming: How organizations learn, innovate, and compete in the knowledge economy.* Jossey Bass.

Edmondson, A. (2018). *The fearless organization : Creating psychological safety in the workplace for learning, innovation, and growth.* Wiley.

Edmondson, A. (2019). *The fearless organization: Creating psychological safety in the workplace for learning, innovation, and growth.* Wiley.

Edmondson, A., Dillon, J.R. and Roloff, K.S. (2007). Three perspectives on team learning: Outcome improvement, task mastery, and group process. *Academy of Management Annals*, 1, 269–314.

Goddard, R.D. and Goddard, Y.L. (2001). A multilevel analysis of the relationship between teacher and collective efficacy in urban schools. *Teaching and Teacher Education.* 17, 807–818.

Goddard, R.G., Hoy, W.K. and Hoy, A.W. (2004). Collective efficacy beliefs: Theoretical developments, empirical evidence, and future directions. *Educational Researcher,* 33(3), 3–13.

Goddard, R. and Salloum, S.J. (2011). Collective efficacy beliefs, organizational excellence, and leadership. In K. S. Cameron and G. Spreitzer (eds), *Oxford handbook for positive organizational scholarship* (pp. 642–650). Oxford University Press. https://doi.org/10.1093/oxfordhb/9780199734610.013.0048

Hall, R and Seidel-Seidel-Horn, I. (2012). *Talk and conceptual change at work. Adequate representation and epistemic stance in a comparative analysis of staitistical consulting and teacher workgroups.* Mind, Culture & Activity, 19 (3); doi: 10.1080/10749039.2012.688233

Hargreaves, A. and O'Connor, M.T. (2018). *Collaborative professionalism: When teaching together means learning for all.* Corwin Press.

Hattie, J. (2018). *Hattie's 2018 updated list of factors related to student achievement; 252 influences and effect size.* https://visible-learning.org/hattie-ranking-influences-effect-sizes-learning-achievement/

Hoy, W.K., Sweetland, S.R. and Smith, P.A. (2002). Toward an organizational model of achievement in high schools: The significance of collective efficacy. *Educational Administration Quarterly,* 38 (1), 77–93.

Jarrell, K. (2017). *Ways of working canvas.* Xplane. https://xplane.com/diverse-teams-and-ways-of-working/

Leonard, D. (2005). *Deep Smarts.* Harvard Business Press.

Lomos, C., Hofman, R. and Bosker, R. (2011). Professional communities and student achievement- a meta-analysis. *School Effectiveness and School Improvement,* 22(2), 121–148. Doi 10.1080/09243453.2010.550467

Schaap, H., Louws, M., Meirink, J., Oolbekkink-Marchand, H., Van Der Want, A., Zuiker, I., Zwart, R. and Meijer, P. (2018). Tensions experienced by teachers when participating in a professional learning community. *Professional Development in Education*; doi: 10.1080/19415257.2018.1547781

Seidel-Horn, I.S. and Kane, B.D. (2015). Opportunities for professional learning in mathematics teacher workgroup conversations: Relationships to instructional expertise. *Journal of the Learning Sciences*, 24 (3), 373–418, doi: 10.1080/10508406.2015.1034865

Seidel-Horn, I.S and Warren-Little, J. (2010). Attending to problems of practice: Routines and resources for professional learning in teachers' workplace interactions. *American Educational Research Journal*, 47 (1), 181–217.

Sutton, P. and Shouse, A. (2019). Tending to the "deep rules" of teacher collaboration. *Teachers College Record*, www.tcrecord.org ID Number: 22844.

The five keys to a successful Google team. https://rework.withgoogle.com/blog/five-keys-to-a-successful-google-team/

Van Lare, M.D. and Brazer, S.D. (2013). Analyzing learning in professional learning communities: A conceptual framework. *Leadership and Policy in Schools*, 12: 374–396. doi: 10.1080/15700763.2013.860463

Vescio, V., Ross, D. and Adams, A. (2008). A review of research on the impact of professional learning communities on teaching practice and student learning. *Teaching and Teacher Education*, 24, 80–91.

Wegner, E., McDermott, R. and Snyder, W. (2002). *Cultivating communities of practice*. Harvard Business School Publishing.

Leading for Capacity Development

Through six chapters, we have considered what emerging, complex contexts demand from schools today, a new model of capacity as learning, and how capacity development requires a coupling of organizational, team, and individual learning to foster more adaptable and agile schools. Only through this coupling of all layers of learning can new knowledge and a competitive advantage for students emerge. We have also briefly reviewed routines leaders can use to help create learning capacity. As a reminder, review the full model in **Figure 7.1**.

While you should have a complete idea by now about what we mean as learning as capacity, this chapter will give some more concrete ideas by exploring two different scenarios using the 5i organizational learning model. This chapter will explore two different uses of the 5i model—one from external demands on Stonybrook High School, and one from an internal need at Stonybrook High School. We will also unpack how leaders use various mindsets, skills, and routines to create new knowledge.

The External Demand Learning Cycle

In this first example of "running the cycle," the leadership and staff at Stonybrook High School use the 5i cycle to begin working toward broader outcomes for student growth.

Leading for Capacity Development

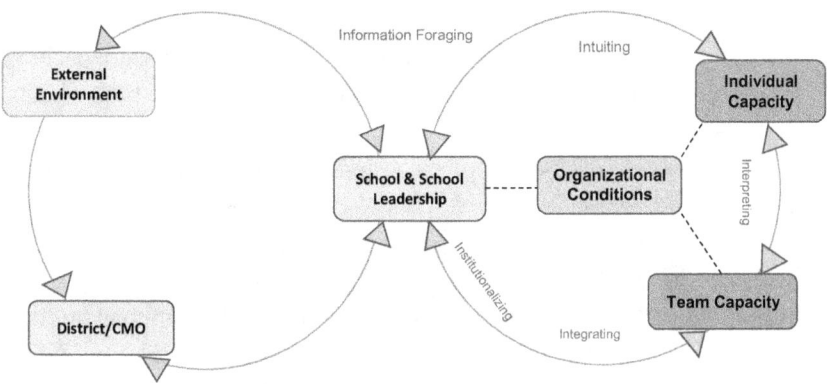

Figure 7.1 A New Model of Learning Capacity in Schools

Cycle 1: Surface Level Learning

1. *Information Foraging.* As a brief reminder, this stage involves doing an environmental or future scan to examine what is happening in the external environment and what a school might learn from it.

After her initial visit to the Stonybrook Food Company, Amanda Lopez knew that her students' future skill needs would be much different from what the typical school developed in its students. At night and on weekends, she scoured articles and books about the future. She saw that while academic knowledge was still valuable, schools needed to focus on more thinking skills, social and emotional skills, and more high-tech career skills. She had a series of ideas in mind but realized as a new principal, more involvement from her staff to come up with a mutual direction would be needed. She knew that developing mindsets around a future orientation and external demands would be needed.

Instead of coming right out and saying change needed to happen, she began to market the need for change through information and stories. Before each faculty meeting, she distributed an article about future work needs that the faculty discussed. Twice a week, she also sent a brief link to an online video about other schools or young people talking about their school needs. She and her assistants also contacted alumni who had just entered the workforce and students in college, interviewed them by video, and recorded them to share what had been missing from their education.

To better set the stage for more in-depth information foraging, Amanda and her leadership team began discussions with the school's department chairs and parent group. Both groups were concerned with getting too far away from a college prep focus but knew that the students at Stonybrook High School would need more than good test scores to be successful. During this time, Amanda also started to work with her leadership team—department heads and assistant principals- on developing the skills around teaming and distributed leadership.

After a quarter of creating a sense of urgency, Ms. Lopez received permission from her superintendent to hire an outside consultant to lead a more in-depth future scanning process. Ms. Lopez had run across a consulting group that specialized in helping schools envision their students' future and decided they were the best firm to help them. The Future of Schools firm assigned a facilitator to Stonybrook high school who met with Amanda, her leadership team, department chairs, and parent volunteers over four full-day meetings. During these facilitated meetings, the facilitator led the whole team through a series of future scanning techniques that looked at workforce trends, societal trends, demographic trends, and technological trends to understand better how these trends were shaping the world. During the last part of each meeting, Ms. Lopez also worked with the team on more teaming and distributed leadership skills she knew they would need as they progressed in this work.

At the end of each meeting, the team synthesized what they had learned and what resonated as the issues and trends that would most impact the students at Stonybrook High School. Team members then presented this synthesis of ideas during staff team meetings held within one week of each full-day meeting. Teachers and school leaders teamed up to present the new learnings and help implication discussions with teachers. During this time, Ms. Lopez also had her tech staff create a shared Google Drive for all staff members to house all of the materials they had started gathering using a tagging feature.

2. *Intuiting.* This stage of the learning process centers around the individual learning level and involves recognizing patterns and insights. During this stage, the framing of the change begins to take shape, and experience, visuals, and metaphors are vital to use. Lakoff and Johnson (2003) discuss the importance of metaphors in that our mental models and beliefs are primarily metaphorical in nature and structure what and how we perceive our world.

As the task force continued to meet with their outside facilitator, their visual presentations began to use more visuals to accompany the discussions. For each topic, they came up with metaphors that would help fellow teachers begin shifting their mindsets. For instance, when discussing workforce preparation changes, they used the metaphor of "Creating the entrepreneurial you" When discussing the trends in technology, they created the metaphor of "technology as a second brain." Overall, the team came up with a sticky message that they all could use to start all meetings: "The future is theirs" became the rallying cry.

During one of the last meetings, teachers on the task force suggested that a series of visits to local businesses would be beneficial. Since they could not release the whole staff, the facilitator arranged a series of recorded webinars with different companies worldwide. During these webinars, individuals gave overviews of their work and responded to each set of drivers –what it meant for their companies and education. The CEO of one large company suggested that students needed extreme agility, more social and emotional skills, and ongoing learning skills to know how to adjust to frequent changes.

At the end of each large staff meeting when new information was shared, Ms.Lopez presented the overall message of "The Future is Theirs" and the metaphor for that area asking people to begin finding patterns and implications from the new information and respond to the metaphor. How does this metaphor help define this set of trends? What makes sense or does not in the metaphor? What are the implications of this metaphor? She also spent time showing staff how teachers conceptually change and the types of supports they would receive. Through this stage, Ms. Lopez and her leadership team created mindsets around sense-making and recognizing insights at every turn.

3. *Interpreting.* As a reminder, this stage uses the wisdom of the team to develop collective meaning, beliefs, and mental models. This stage utilizes teaming as learning, requiring a distributed leadership model and excellent facilitation skills, and a sense of positivity. Mindsets at this stage center on creating meaning around experience.

During this stage, Ms. Lopez began to create more opportunities for distributed leadership by letting her leadership team members take on more responsibility. At the same time, she worked to develop their facilitation skills. Using their staff PLC's, teams led by teachers began the interpretation process and decided on which of the studied areas they thought would benefit their students the most. Team leaders gathered feedback and discussed each area's pros and cons and its impact on students and teachers. After much consideration, the leadership team decided that social–emotional learning was the first area to pursue as they had heard again and again how necessary these skills were in the external environment and how they aided academic learning.

Once this decision occurred, the leadership team started a document called "The Future is Theirs: SEL at Stonybrook High School," created as the overall, shared mental model for this area. This document, which rested in the shared Google Drive, was created to develop coherence and instructional guidance around this initiative. The document, written by a leadership team member, clarified what was meant by SEL and the various skills, dispositions, and qualities they wanted to help develop in their students.

Now that there was a prevailing direction, the leadership team decided that the intuiting and interpreting stages needed various learning methods. Various book studies formed, and online courses were found so teachers could learn at their own pace when they had time. PLC's were also used to help understand and create the connections between academic content and social-emotional learning. New learnings were captured and shared through the various teams, and the shared Google Drive became a repository of these ideas.

4. *Integrating.* At this stage of the learning process, the strategy moves from learning about the idea to learning from using the idea. This stage works in tandem with the interpretation stage in that trying something out, learning from success and failure, and learning from the trials helps to create new knowledge. In the lean startup language, this is the build, measure, learn integration of these two stages. Essential leadership mindsets in this stage include creating feedback loops for adaptability and connecting people and teams.

Most staff members had a growing knowledge base around SEL and its importance for students. However, Ms. Lopez and her leadership team knew there was a big difference between knowing and doing. To help overcome this, Ms. Lopez and her assistant principals had been studying the process of design thinking, and one AP took it upon himself to become an expert in this area. The administrative team introduced design thinking to the broader leadership team to create small trials of ideas to create new knowledge about how SEL worked with their students. Rather than focus on individual teachers, teams were charged with coming up with a design idea together to try out in multiple classrooms. This method became a knowledge creation strategy. This strategy did not preclude borrowing ideas from other sources, but the leadership team wanted to start moving ideas into practice. The school's advisory period was designated as the primary space for this learning form, but other techniques and models were chosen for use during regular class time.

During this stage, the smaller teams also moved back and forth between their trials in the integration stage back to interpreting the impact on students. New knowledge aided iterations of designs, and the shared mental models were adjusted, defended, and surfaced through these trials. This process is the real purpose behind feedback and knowledge building in that teams tried something, collected data on its use, and took that data back to their teams to make sense of it and adjust their next trials. These trials were shared through the leadership team, informal discussions between teachers, and codified in the Google Drive.

From these trials, one area Ms. Lopez and her assistant principals looked at carefully was the trials' design and the measurement of impact. By analyzing the codified documents, Ms. Lopez and her assistant principals saw that these areas needed more support, so they provided extra scaffolding for specific teams and worked with the leadership team to figure out better ways to measure impact.

Always concerned with growing a positive culture, Ms. Lopez and her other assistant principal began working with the broader leadership team on creating a positive culture—not as some separate set of tasks or initiatives but as part of their overall work with SEL. Specifically, they worked with the other leaders on forming more positive relationships, positive meaning, and positive energy. Ms. Lopez and her AP created a tool bank for the other leaders to use, and use what they called flash surveys—2–3 question surveys—in each meeting about the relationships and energy at their team meetings. These data were aggregated for any signs of concerns on teams and overall as a school.

5. *Institutionalizing*. In this stage of the learning process, the learning and knowledge building that has occurred becomes a part of the school's routines and culture if supported and developed well. In this stage, leaders develop mindsets around crafting coherence and accountability.

Leading for Capacity Development

> During the last few weeks of the school year, Ms. Lopez commended her leadership team on the learning and work they had done the past year. However, she noted that there was still lots of work ahead as some of the team designs were not that impactful, and staff members still had lots of questions. To help deepen their knowledge, the leadership team had found a summer conference to attend. They formulated the questions they and their teams still had to investigate during the conference. The team discussed and analyzed their level of understanding and comfort with team learning, supporting individual beliefs, and using design thinking. They also began to discuss ways of creating coherence and accountability across all teams.

Cycle 2: Deepening the Learning

During the second year of the Social-Emotional Learning initiative at Stonybrook High School, the leadership team worked to deepen the learning around social-emotional development.

> 1. Information Foraging. With a well-formulated sense of the questions their staff was asking about SEL, the leadership team from Stonybrook High School had a definite plan for how to approach their summer conference. The team had plans for which sessions to attend and the materials for which they were looking. After each day, the team met by the pool, debriefed the sessions, and formulated more questions. One of the teachers had met a university professor who met with the team one afternoon, and another teacher had found a couple of good books on SEL that she thought would be useful for the school.
>   During their last debrief, one of the assistant principals took notes about what they had learned and the next steps for the SEL initiative and sent it to all staff members. Similarly, Ms. Lopez had her tech team create a web page of best SEL websites, so teachers had a one-stop page for all of these resources.
> 2. Intuiting. When teachers returned to school from summer break, the leadership team had created a half-day workshop around their

questions. Instead of everybody receiving the same information, the team had created a "choose your own professional" learning day based on personalized needs. Team members did some sessions; some sessions were done online. Some provided one-on-one coaching, and some allowed more guided design thinking to happen. At the close of this half-day, Ms. Lopez took the staff back through "The Future is Theirs: SEL at Stonybrook High School" guide and split the document by teams so that they could update it to resurface their initial mental models.

The next day, the staff spent another half day with an outside expert on the pedagogy of deliberate practice for students' SEL skills and how to help students improve through reflection. Using the CAMCC model as their guide for individual conceptual change and surveys of individual efficacy, the leadership team sat down at the end of the workshop, reviewed the data, and decided on each departmental team's next support steps.

3. Interpreting/4. Integrating. As the school year began, the school PLC's continued to meet weekly around their SEL initiative using new ideas and designing new ways to approach teaching SEL skills to their students. Teachers searched for and found ideas vetted by their teams and then shared with the entire team. The teams continued to discuss the impact on students. Ms. Lopez and her assistant principals continued to stress the idea of "build, measure, learn" and tried to attend as many PLC meetings as possible to learn from their teachers and stress the idea of impact.

During this time, the leadership team also began to redesign the shared Google drive layout, so documents could more easily be found. The leadership team also began asking that Ms. Lopez and her assistants spend more time in classrooms during the advisory period and offer collective feedback. Large-scale survey data were also collected and reviewed by the leadership team, showing that students' sense of belonging increased as did belief in a growth mindset. Lower areas like self-regulation were discussed, and new designs were created to help students with this skill. Quarterly, the collective efficacy of staff was measured as was coherence around the SEL initiative.

Leading for Capacity Development

A positive culture's supporting role continued through Ms. Lopez and her AP, who continued to work on strategies for positive climate, meaning, relationships, and energy. These strategies were used in large group meetings, team meetings, and in smaller one on one meetings again not as a separate set of ideas but as an integral part of the SEL learning and knowledge creation.

5. Institutionalizing. At the end of the second year, the SEL initiative was firmly centered in the advisory time. About 30% of teachers had begun using SEL ideas during their regular class periods. While some hard-core academic teachers still grumbled about being too touchy-feely, most acknowledged they felt a more profound sense of connection to their students.

During their last leadership team meeting for the year, the team acknowledged their successes. They also discussed what more they needed to learn and figure out as they created their knowledge base. Reviewing Google Drive for new knowledge added, they saw that over 80% of teachers had contributed some new idea or resource. Reviewing data, they saw gains on student self-perception around the areas they had targeted for the second semester but still saw needs in specific competencies. They also knew that averages masked some students' sense of development, so figuring out which students needed more support became a big topic of discussion. Overall, the team saw hope that their hard work helped many students gain a different set of skills that would benefit them their whole lives.

Exploring the Leadership Mindsets, Skills, and Routines Used

Because this is a fictional vignette, it is hard to determine how much actual time would be needed to get to institutionalization or how quickly a school can move to a new learning area. We did want to note, however, the cyclical nature of the learning work using the flywheel metaphor (Collins, 2019). The first cycle began the process, and as new questions and ideas rose, new learning occurred, which pushed the flywheel further and faster. By having a clarity of purpose, coherence in knowledge building and learning can be more targeted and specific. Multiple strands of development were also co-occurring during these two cycles. As the school was engaging in the learning around SEL, they were also developing conditions for effective teaming, distributed leadership, and design thinking. Note that these examples, do not necessarily show linear effects, but rather are systemic in nature. As teams and individuals learn about one area, they are also embedded in another area that develops simultaneously. The conditions both cause and are caused by learning.

Specific to the conditions, mindsets, and routines used during these cycles, Ms. Lopez began focusing heavily on gaining clarity of purpose, creating effective teams, and a distributed leadership model. She also began to help create a different set of mindsets or mental models and beliefs about what the future was demanding from their students for her leadership team. During the intuiting stage or stage of individual learning, the use of metaphors and visuals helped dislodge old mental models and create new beliefs. Specific kernels of teaching practice were tried and refined over time to focus on conceptual change, and systematic processing was built to help support these new beliefs. Design thinking helped create a vicarious information source during the interpretation phase to create more collective efficacy by using replay and revision strategies. Team leaders trained in creating psychological safety through the design process. Collective and individual efficacy surveys were used on an ongoing basis to provide extra support to teams, and knowledge management processes became more prevalent as staff interest grew.

In contrast to other school leadership models, what Ms. Lopez and her team did could be considered as leading and supporting the broader knowledge-building strategy. However, three crucial considerations merit attention. First, she used her official authority to begin or catalyze the need toward clarity of purpose: specifically, around future demands. Second, Ms. Lopez and her assistant principals knew that they needed to develop a distributed leadership model based on the leading of learning with everything else. Third, Ms. Lopez and her team focused on the learning process at the individual, team, and organizational levels. Because they were novices about SEL, like their teachers, they realized that a more significant role was to enable their staff to understand and develop the elements at each level of learning to create more agile and adaptable learning.

Last, this example shows the role of learning agility—a concept discussed in Chapter 1—and how this condition support creates organizational learning. First, we know that organizational learning has occurred when created knowledge becomes institutionalized in the school's routines, systems, strategy, and culture. In this example, the teaching of SEL started to become a part of the advisory routine, as did the use of design thinking methods to interpret and integrate new ideas. Similarly, by embedding features of positive cultures into all aspects of group and team meetings, these strategies and routines started to become part of the overall culture.

Second, in this example, we can see that Knowledge Management consisted of both a technical and social dynamic. By creating a shared Google drive, teachers could codify, find, and store knowledge-based artifacts from which others could learn. Using team learning, individuals could surface their tacit knowledge about their changes and make it more explicit for others.

Third, in this example, we can also witness how the concepts of dynamic capability and absorptive capacity interact to create organizational learning. As a reminder, dynamic capability refers to the school's ability to continually create, integrate, and reconfigure new resources for competitive advantage (Vera et al., 2011). In this example, the school used information foraging techniques to scan the school's external environment for needs not being met. When acted upon, this knowledge gave their students a more competitive advantage for the future by developing broader, more aligned outcomes that better prepare them for the external environment.

Over time as the systems and routines for learning deepen, dynamic capability builds. This dynamic capability also enhances the absorptive capacity, defined as the ability to assimilate and exploit new knowledge. In conjunction, realized absorptive capacity reflects the school's ability to leverage the knowledge that has been absorbed (Vera et al., 2011). "The more absorptive capacity an organization has, the more it will benefit from engagement with new knowledge in the future" (Farrell et al., 2019).

As a broader concept of learning agility, the more dynamic a school is in looking to the external environment, the more absorptive capacity builds, and the ability to utilize the knowledge gained increases. These conditions rely on the learning systems and knowledge management used in a school that eventually leads to organizational learning. Over time, these dynamic interactions lead to changes in organizational routines and processes (e.g., organizational learning that helps create an innovative school). While this may be conceptually difficult, suffice it to say that the better knowledge/learning strategy leaders can create, the better competitive advantage it gives its students.

Internal Demand Learning Cycle

Much of what has driven school improvement has come from state and federal accountability demands in the last decade. By testing all students using a similar test and sending schools data, state-driven accountability policies assume schools have enough capacity to use this information to determine the necessary changes. However, this is not always the case. In the next example, the Stonybrook math department uses improvement science techniques as their knowledge/learning strategy to create an internal cycle of learning involving individuals, the department team, and the school organization.

1. *Information foraging.* Delberta Jones, the head of the math department, was a 23-year veteran of teaching high school math and was a deliberate and intentional learner. She had numerous discussions with Ms. Lopez, her principal, about new ideas for math teaching and trying to prevent students' math failure. The hair would bristle on her neck when students would tell her they hated math or could not do math. She knew this came from poor instruction and a fixed mindset. Her goal was to get 100% of Stonybrook's students to pass the state math test at the first attempt by paying more attention to student beliefs and progressive pedagogy. Her colleagues were not always as enthused.

   Ms. Jones was a voracious researcher and was always finding new ideas and methods. She had a different vision for math teaching and learning and saw it as not only as a useful way to think about the world but also as a social justice issue. Ms. Jones belonged to national and state organizations and was always attending conferences to gain new ideas. Her fellow teachers knew she walked her talk and would often come to watch her teach. She had lately started researching the idea of Improvement

Science and had been given money to attend a virtual course on this method. As she went through the course, she began to see how this method could help deal with some of the intractable problems she and her colleagues faced.

2. *Intuiting*. At the next departmental meeting, Delberta decided to go out on a limb and share her latest learnings with her colleagues from the course on Improvement Science she had just finished. She had been encouraged by Ms. Lopez and her administrative team to understand this process and use it to help improve the Algebra I course passage rate. She had also been encouraged to be very explicit about new math teaching ideas so the math department could envision with her what the department could become.

At the department meeting, Ms. Jones shared the origins of Improvement Science and how it was used in schools across the US. She told the story of how using these techniques at the community college level had increased developmental passing rates. She also explained the idea of small experiments and the use of data to know if the change was an improvement. She then told the story of Ramy, a student who had been an A–B student in math at their school but at college got stuck in the remedial track and never got out. Her emotional plea was to help the Ramy's of their school.

While she acknowledged this would require a collective effort, she told her colleagues they were already using cycles like this in their teaching. It probably was just not formalized. From Ms. Lopez, she had learned that, at this stage, teachers needed a chance to begin making sense of the new ideas and to distill some patterns. She asked them to think of other students like Ramy and why they thought they got stuck when they went off to college. After a compelling discussion, Ms. Jones asked if anybody wanted to explore Improvement Science with her. Six of the 12 teachers said they would be willing, the other six hesitated but said they would start if the data showed they were making a difference.

To start, Ms. Jones gave the six teachers a collection of readings on new math pedagogy, student mindsets about math, and Improvement Science to help ground them. They met after school for the next few weeks to begin making sense of what this process was about and how it could help them.

3. *Interpreting.* As this group continued to meet, Ms. Jones and Ms. Lopez worked together to formulate the next steps, learn about Improvement Science, and how it could foster learning at multiple levels. To create a shared mental model, Ms. Jones and the other teachers discussed the most impactful problem on passage rates. They collaborated to create what is known as a driver diagram, which is a tool used in Improvement Science to develop a theory of improvement. Driver diagrams try to capture those elements within a system that work together to create the desired result. As their primary aim, the team decided to improve Algebra I's student passage rates by 10% yearly. Their overall driver diagram listed primary drivers, such as prior learning, student persistence, and teaching/learning strategies, as primary influences on student learning. They initially chose productive persistence as their problem of practice, and both Ms. Jones and Ms. Lopez worked with them on developing change ideas to turn into kernels of practice.

4. *Integrating.* The primary method of turning ideas into action in Improvement Science is through the creation and use of Plan-Do-Study-Act (PDSA cycles). PDSA cycles are small, short experiments that attempt to improve one of the primary drivers and act as the primary routine for individual and team learning. They are part of the "disciplined inquiry" principle in which teachers decide on the specific change and measure its impact. Over multiple iterations like in design thinking, knowledge emerges about how best to improve a problem.

At first, all teachers created a standard PDSA cycle based on student persistence techniques. By talking to students about specific strategies, teachers began to see improved persistence around harder math problems. Numerous cycles led to modify the strategies, and over time, individual teachers began to create their own PDSA cycles based on their problems of practice. Prediction was a critical step in that teachers would predict what they think might happen with the change idea and compare it to what happened. Conceptual change in teachers' discussion was becoming more apparent, as was the sense of collective efficacy from surveys given. Highly refined change ideas were written up, shared with others, and placed into the shared Google drive for all to access.

As the department chair, Ms. Jones became a conduit of ideas with her teachers. When they raised an issue, she would have them filter the problem through the driver diagram and help them find resources for new ideas to try. Department meetings became focused on sharing new knowledge and deepening an understanding of measuring their change ideas' impact. Over time, more and more teachers began to see the power of this form of learning and started to learn from their peers even though they did not create their own PDSA cycle. Ms. Jones worked with teachers not only to create the PDSA plans but to help them create associated deliberate practice routines that the teachers videotaped and shared with Ms. Jones for reflective feedback.

5. *Institutionalizing.* Over two years, the math department at Stonybrook became a team focused on learning from their actions. While they continued to integrate PLC structures, they used PDSA cycles within that structure when new problems arose. Their driver diagram worked as the central set of ideas for their department and was modified as they tackled more difficult challenges. The driver diagram helped create coherence for their work, and any newly hired teacher into the department was expected to know it by heart. Specific challenges were developed and agreed to by the whole team. These challenges moved from critical conversations around accelerating students who were behind to using more culturally responsive methods. They added to the shared Google Drive that contained PDSA plans, shared lesson plans, and even videos. Over time, teacher beliefs and mindsets began to shift about students and their capabilities, and collective efficacy measures proved this out.

Exploring the Leadership Mindsets, Skills, and Routines Used

Schools and departments often use a linear process of "adopt, attack and abandon" (Rohanna, 2018) when trying to improve. In this familiar pattern, schools or departments choose an idea and use it without adapting the idea through learning. People quickly attack it then abandon it, throwing it on the pile of previous reform ideas. To change the maladaptive pattern of adopt, attack, and abandon, the math department's leadership took a different approach by using Improvement Science to support individual, team, and organizational learning.

In this example, specific ideas from our capacity-building model deserve attention. First, PDSA cycles provide an ongoing focus on interpretation and integration. Iterations for each cycle focused on deepening the strategies and techniques used. Each time the team met to create the next iteration of practice provided an efficacy sense of information by providing vicarious experience in planning and social persuasion to try out new change ideas. Taping lessons for feedback also helped to create a mastery experience for teachers trying out the change ideas. Over time, these cycles helped create a deeper understanding of the driver of productive persistence. These cycles and the driver diagram also created the condition of instructional clarity and coherence in that the primary drivers provided a way to understand all of the factors that can influence student math achievement.

Second, by developing the PDSA ideas together, teachers could challenge their own beliefs in a supportive environment and develop individual efficacy. By creating psychological safety and a process of team creation, collective efficacy developed over time. The use of the PDSA plans created and fostered new learning, which added to the team's collective IQ.

Ms. Jones benefitted from being part of the distributed leadership network at her school and receiving ongoing support as her department leader. By understanding individual learning elements like expertise, beliefs, self-efficacy, and conceptual change, Ms. Jones could help support members of her department. Moreover, by learning about teaming, team learning skills, team psychological safety, and collective efficacy, Ms. Jones could help her team learn from their actions and create new knowledge.

Similar to the whole school example explored above, this departmental example also shows how the choice of Improvement Science can lead to organizational learning. Over time and numerous cycles, new techniques to address student persistence became routine in the department showing organizational learning had occurred. Second, the discussion of the impact on change ideas was a form of knowledge management that eventually became part of the shared Google drive.

Third, by continuously searching for external ideas, Ms. Jones and the other teachers created more dynamic capability around new ideas that quickly became a competitive advantage for their students. As discussed in Chapter 1, absorptive capacity defines as a school's ability to use external knowledge by

(a) recognizing and understanding valuable new knowledge;
(b) assimilating this new knowledge through learning; and
(c) exploiting or using this knowledge to create even more new knowledge (Lane et al. 2006)

By using Improvement Science for learning, teachers could quickly iterate change ideas and capitalize on this new knowledge almost immediately. All these departmental conditions benefited because of deliberate and productive learning processes and systems.

Diagnosing Your School

As in previous chapters, to fully understand this new model for capacity development, leaders need to understand how various learning systems and elements work together in each stage of the 5i method of organizational learning (see **Figure 7.2** below). By understanding the complete model, note how individual and team learning systems can lead to organizational learning. By using the Learning Capacity Diagnostic, you can determine which learning level and element may need the most support.

Team Considerations

A CEO once suggested, "If the world is moving faster outside your organization than inside it, the end is near." While we do not believe any public school will end, we believe that schools and school systems need a clear knowledge-building strategy using organizational learning to become more adaptable and agile. Students today, especially those who are most disenfranchised, need a competitive advantage. As these examples show,

Stage of 5i method	Primary Learning Level to engage	Primary Element to consider/develop	Organizational Condition to consider/develop
Information foraging	Team	Teaming Team learning Psych safety	Clarity of purpose Distributed leadership Positive cultures Innovation processes Knowledge management
Intuiting	Individual	Beliefs Conceptual change	Clarity of purpose Distributed leadership Positive cultures Innovation processes Knowledge management
Interpreting	Individual Team	Conceptual change Beliefs Deliberate practice Team learning Psychological safety Efficacy	Coherence Distributed leadership Positive cultures Innovation processes Knowledge management
Integrating	Team	Efficacy Teaming Team learning Psychological safety	Coherence Distributed leadership Positive cultures Innovation processes Knowledge management
Institutionalizing	Team Organizational	Teaming Team learning Efficacy	Coherence Distributed leadership Positive cultures Innovation processes Knowledge management

Figure 7.2 Diagnostic Guide for Building Learning Capacity

running the organizational learning cycles and developing the conditions for organizational, team, and individual learning happens.

As we have previously discussed, school capacity is a complex adaptive system and requires an interaction between the external and internal worlds led by leaders focused on learning. After taking the diagnostic, as a team, think more about these cases and consider these questions.

1. So now, how are you defining capacity?
2. What differences do you see between the two processes used?

3. How do you explain the relationships between the stages of the 5i method, learning system, learning element, and organizational conditions?
4. How do they feed one another?
5. Which of the 5i stages are most pronounced in your school? Least?
6. Why is an ongoing focus on the external environment important?
7. How might you prevent too early of an interpretation by individuals? Why is that important?
8. How might you stop the adopt, attack, and abandon cycle?
9. Why are cycles necessary for institutionalization?
10. Why might you choose one overall learning process over the other?

References

Collins, J. (2019). *Turning the flywheel: A monograph to accompany good to great.* Harper Business.

Farrell, C.C., Coburn, C.E. and Chong, S. (2019). Under what conditions do school districts learn from external partners? The role of absorptive capacity. *American Educational Research Journal*, 56 (3), 955–994. Doi: 10.3102/0002831218808219

Lakoff, G. and Johnson, M. (2003). *Metaphors we live by.* University of Chicago Press.

Lane, P.J., Koka, BR and Pathak, S. (2006). The reification of absorptive capacity: A critical review and rejuvenation of the construct. *Academy of Management Review*, 31 (4), 833–863.

Rohanna, K. (2018). *Preparing schools to successfully participate in networked improvement communities: A case study of year 1 of a math instructional network.* Unpublished doctoral dissertation. University of California, Los Angeles.

Vera, D., Crossan, M. and Apaydin, M. (2011). A framework for integrating organizational learning, knowledge, capabilities, and absorptive capacity. In Easterby-Smith, M. and Lyles, M., (eds), *Handbook of organizational learning and knowledge management*, (2nd edn 153–180). Wiley.

8 Back to the Future

After four years as principal at Stonybrook High School, Amanda Lopez had much about which to be proud. After making it through the Covid-19 crisis and extended protests around racial inequities in the community, Stonybrook High School emerged as a much different educational institution. With the Covid-19 turmoil and so many students behind, the faculty had decided to develop a competency-based model using the hybrid learning model to focus on helping students develop more self-direction and extended support for students most in need. Faculty had also decided to examine racial and socioeconomic inequities in their school to determine where unconscious biases showed up in their climate and academic program and had found many they were willing to examine.

As she stood on the balcony overlooking the student commons at her school during the lunch period, she noted the banner from her state's education department for the most improved school. As Amanda watched her students eat, text, and laugh, she thought back to the early days. Her school seemed like a collection of individuals going in a hundred different directions. She thought back to all of the hard work her AP's had done and other members of her leadership team. Amanda could honestly say that her school had made rapid improvements by distributing her leadership and helping others develop theirs. She also thought back to the initial push back from her teachers around "all this learning." Still, she now admired how much they had learned through the school's connection between individual, team, and organizational learning. Not only were test scores up, but SEL measures showed student growth in this area, and student climate surveys showed that more students of color felt like they had a connection to the school.

More future-oriented skills of creativity, critical thinking, and communication were highly evident in course assignments. More personalization was happening for students under a competency-based system, with students learning more about developing their agency. More future-oriented CTE programs had also been implemented, and a new STEM career academy was opening at Stonybrook next fall. The school's new hive or knowledge management system was the center of all their improvement and learning work and was used daily by her staff. As the bell went to signal time for extended advisory time, Ms. Lopez walked back toward her office to review the agenda for her Future Scanning Committee. They had plenty more to discuss.

We began this book with an overarching premise: To meet our society's increasing complexity, we have to update our mental models around schools and organize around continuous organizational learning to become more agile and adaptable. We also explained that these different mental models need to be supported by a new model for organizational capacity based on coupling individual and team learning, leading to organizational learning. We defined this learning capacity again as

Capacity as a noun means the set of defined processes and conditions that help a school organize for learning at the individual, team, and organizational level within a central purpose. Over time, this learning becomes a resource that can be drawn upon to improve agility and adaptability.

Capacity Development as a verb means using processes to promote interaction for learning at the individual, team, and organizational level to build more dynamic agility and adaptability.

Throughout this book, we have argued that schools need a continual learning and knowledge-building strategy to meet the new set of problems they face today, since few solutions currently exist. Organizational knowledge building is a research-proven construct and provides a vital resource and source of competitive advantage for any organization (Vera et al., 2011). In a sense, we tried to articulate the need for a new operating system based on learning for knowledge building versus the typical "adopt, attack, and abandon" pattern of response many schools have used in the past (Rohana, 2018).

We described the outcome of this new "operating system" as learning agility and adaptability. As a brief reminder, this concept means the fundamental speed of knowledge building and the belief that this new knowledge is useful. As a reminder, learning agility and adaptability combines four interrelated concepts.

- *Absorptive capacity*: The condition that allows a school to absorb and leverage external expertise.
- *Dynamic capability*: Knowledge is a resource that can change over time and centers on the speed or dynamic of reconfiguring knowledge into new assets that a school can use (Della Corte and Del Gaudio, 2012).
- *Knowledge Management*: The condition that explains how knowledge is created, disseminated, and stored for ongoing use in organizations.
- *Knowledge Building:* A process that takes place in a well-defined problem space and produces knowledge based on open dialogue and consideration to help build a common mental models (Bereiter and Scardamalia, 2014).

Over time, learning agility and adaptability materialize as the new operating system for schools as learning capacity develops. This new state is about the degree to which a school creates new knowledge, the speed at which it leverages that knowledge, and how it gets further used.

So why is a new operating system necessary? In Chapter 1, we attempted to lay out the argument that schools often inherit society's stressors and have to contend with four complex contexts if they are to deliver on their promise for society. These four contexts include:

- *Covid-19 crisis*: At the time this book was being finalized, we had entered the twelfth month of the Covid crisis with little relief on the horizon. Widening gaps in learning appeared and trying to recreate the traditional model of school online exacerbated many problems of the traditional model of schooling.
- *Increased focus on equity*: Calls for a more equitable society for people of color continued to grow in their intensity, including the stoppage

of play in many professional sports leagues in the summer of 2020. As demographics in the United States continue to shift, calls for more equity for students will continue to be a context to which schools must respond.

- *Future drivers*: Ongoing shifts like technology and artificial intelligence in our society will continue to drive us further into a fourth industrial revolution. These shifts have already started and will continue to create contexts that schools must acknowledge to prepare students to become more agile and adaptable throughout their lives.
- *New organizational forms and leadership*: Last, demands have intensified for more humane and people-centered organizations focused on engagement and empowerment. Organizational forms that still use command and control structures find it more difficult to be fast and agile enough to meet the onslaught of these demands and help people find a more profound purpose in their work as educators (Corbin, 2017). These demands will require us to rethink the "command and control" organizational forms we are used to and move toward a more networked, team-focused structure.

If those contexts aren't enough, a fifth and radically different context, not previously discussed, that schools must adapt to is the new world of work. Emerging data on the new world of work suggests students now in school will experience a very different work environment.

Talent and learning demands change in each generation and revolution. We have moved from an agrarian society where home and work were combined to the second revolution, which focused on manufacturing and an occupational identity separate from home. The third revolution focused on STEM to build the infrastructure for the Fourth industrial revolution. However, these shifts do not come easily for most schools or school systems as most of the schools' organizational structure and culture rest on implicit standards of success and prior generational models.

Today, however, the current operating system is crumbling beneath our feet as industries change, colleges become more expensive, and automation proliferates. Experts now estimated that by 2030, 75–375 million workers may need to switch occupations due to automation (Ford, 2013). A recent report from McKinsey suggested that available technologies could replace 45% of current human work. Another researcher says this number could be as high as 75% by the end of the century. Other data estimates that 65% of the jobs today's elementary students will have do not yet exist, and students today will have seventeen jobs across a total of five industries (Ford, 2013).

These changes will require extreme learning agility for all workers in the future (Friedman, 2016). McGowan and Shipley (2017) concur by suggesting that "In our efforts to improve education in this country, we may be shooting ourselves in the foot. We are myopically focused on proving learning, but that which can be proven is also that which is easy to automate."

The era of uncertainty in which we now exist requires a different form of talent development for a different world of work that is not apparent in many of today's schools. For instance, in a recent survey, only 52% of adults thought high-school students today are prepared to enter the workforce, and only 15% of high-school students believed they were career ready (Kauffman Foundation, 2019).

Because of these and numerous other factors, the paradigm of preparing students for college as the only end destination requires a significant shift in the role and purpose of K-12 education. Many current occupations do not have durability in today's world, so agility, flexibility, and constant learning are required. Employers and adults are asking for more skills such as time management, self-management, communication skills to be prioritized, along with the ability to tolerate, control, and express emotions. Similarly, both adults and students do not believe schools are preparing them for entrepreneurship (Kauffman Foundation, 2019). According to McGowan and Shipley (2017):

> This new work mindset will require a heightened level of self-awareness about one's ability and methods for learning, adaptation, and value creation. This is a shift from learning to do to learning in order to continuously learn and adapt. This is a shift from storing stocks of knowledge to working in flows of emerging knowledge with a trans-disciplinary mindset of human and technology collaboration. This is analogous to learning to master a single instrument versus learning to conduct an orchestra.

Today, and as we advance into the twenty-first century, the velocity of change due to many factors is exponentially increasing, meaning that jobs are quickly displaced, and new ideas emerge daily requiring new learning. This exponential growth suggests strongly that today's students will continuously dip in and out of work and have to remain engaged in learning to stay ahead. We used to think that the number one factor for getting ahead was getting a college degree; this still may help, but will not be enough moving forward. Instead, the idea of learning agility and agency throughout one's life will be the number one factor that separates the employable from the not. But these are not the skills focused on in a test-driven accountability mindset.

In the past, we became educated; now, we must continue working and learning and adapting to remain educated. For example, in a recent economic study, 94% of new work was in the alternative category meaning temporary, gig work, or project-based (Katz and Krueger, 2016).

McGowan and Shipley (2020) describe this new paradigm well when they say:

> We need to recognize that as we leave the third and enter the fourth industrial revolution our systems of learning – that is, codifying knowledge into a curriculum, then transferring that predetermined knowledge to accepting students so that they can become productive workers – can't support a rapidly changing world where new knowledge is continuously created and new skills are required to capture opportunity.

In other words, we used to focus on developing individual expertise in a narrow area. Now we need to build the agility to develop expertise as new ideas and needs emerge. The battle between a stock of knowledge to rely on and the flow of ever-increasing knowledge requires educators and schools to model this process more deliberately. With these new constraints in our economy, schools will need to help students develop organizing mental models for content and unlearn and shed old skills and become more aware of emerging trends.

Students will need to develop a different operating system based more on purpose, passion, and an ever-increasing reservoir of knowledge and skills. What, then, are these fundamental literacies? We are starting to see some models at a few universities and colleges, and some new K-12 models have also emerged.

For example, one way to help students prepare for this uncertain future is to focus on developing an Agile Mindset. "Simply put, the Agile Mindset is a set of intellectual tools that enables students to look at situations from various perspectives in a way that will give them a competitive edge at work, and in life" (Agile Mindset, 2017). These tools include:

- empathy or the skill of working with others to identify new problems or needs;
- divergent thinking or coming up with new solutions for problems or needs;
- entrepreneurial outlook or creating and capturing value from solutions; and
- social and emotional intelligence to help students work collaboratively and learn how to adapt and manage transitions.

Similarly, the Next Generation Learning Challenge (NGLC) has created a framework that utilizes four large domains to group 20 competencies. These include:

- habits of success or inter and intrapersonal skills necessary to succeed;
- creative know-how or developing in the areas of critical thinking, communication, collaboration, and creativity;
- content knowledge or a more focused core along with interdisciplinary and CTE skills; and
- wayfinding abilities or the ability to navigate and adapt as students progress through life (NGLC Framework).

In sum, the emerging future is putting severe pressures on schools' operating systems as we know them. With these pressures growing exponentially, the ability to prepare students through traditional models to adapt and adjust continually has become increasingly limited. As we have stated numerous times, schools need a new operating system based on these economic realities and complex contexts in which they exist.

A New Model of Learning Capacity in Schools

This book presented a simple yet profound idea. If we need to develop a new operating system for our schools, then the adults in our schools need to create a new operating system based on learning as capacity. As we have explored throughout, we started with a base definition of capacity:

Capacity as a noun means the set of defined processes and conditions that help a school organize for learning at the individual, team, and organizational level around a central purpose. Over time this learning builds new knowledge and becomes a resource that can be drawn upon to improve agility and adaptability.

Capacity Development as a verb means using processes to promote interaction for learning at the individual, team, and organizational level to build more dynamic agility and adaptability.

To understand this model of capacity as learning, we first explored capacity as organizational conditions noting that these conditions help develop and are developed by other forms of learning and their elements. For capacity to develop over time, school leaders need to attend to the influence of these conditions on learning, including:

- clarity of purpose;
- coherence;
- distributed leadership;
- positive cultures; and
- learning agility.

Next, we explored organizational capacity as organizational processes, explicitly using the 5i organizational learning model. The 5i model and unique learning processes act as the overarching learning stages that help leaders organize the necessary generative learning to build knowledge. To develop in-depth capacity at the school level, school leaders need to utilize these specific processes:

- The 5i model includes:
    - information foraging
    - intuiting
    - interpreting
    - integrating
    - institutionalizing
- Special learning processes, including:
    - improvement science
    - design thinking.

Third, we explored the role of individual learning, noting that individual learning relies heavily on the individual teacher's mental models and beliefs. Individual learning also rests on the ideas of deliberate practice to develop expertise. To develop this level as a form of capacity, school leaders need to understand these specific elements, including:

- expertise and the role of deliberate practice;
- mental models and beliefs;
- self-efficacy; and
- conceptual change

Fourth, we explored the primary source of learning in this new model of capacity building- teaming. We noted that teams sit between the individual and organizational levels of learning and that teams in many industries, including education, have become the de facto structure for how the work of learning gets accomplished. For leaders to utilize this structure to develop capacity, they must attend to these elements in this learning system:

- teaming;
- team learning;
- psychological safety; and
- collective efficacy.

In sum, this new model brings together many different lines of thought and inquiry around the one fundamental answer/response to the era of uncertainty: capacity as learning and knowledge building (see **Figure 8.1**).

The Leaders' New Mindsets and Skills

The primary focus for this new model of capacity development is on learning and knowledge building for enhanced agility and adaptability. As Fullan (2011) so eloquently states, "Learning is the work," and leading this learning is educational leaders' work in the twenty-first century. To reiterate why, in complex knowledge environments like schools, new problems emerge in which there is little or no knowledge base of answers to apply.

Back to the Future

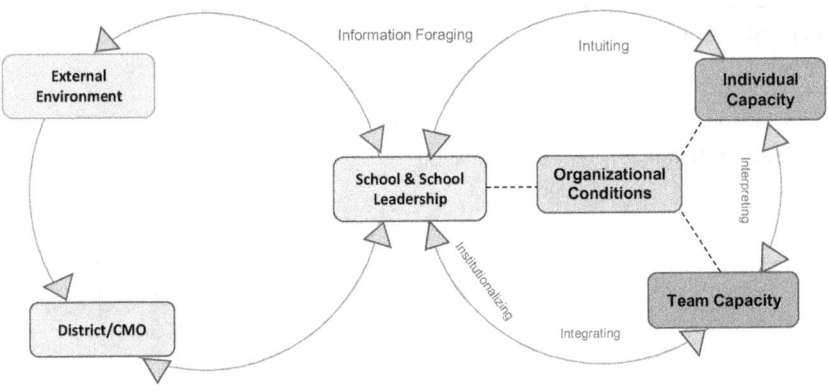

Figure 8.1 A New Model for Learning Capacity in Schools

Therefore, more generative forms of learning need to be used to create or generate new solutions.

To help learning and create this knowledge, we have detailed a model that links individual, team, and organizational learning to understand how capacity builds. We have also explored new mindsets and skills leaders in a distributed model will need (see **Figure 8.2**). While we believe numerous frameworks for modern leadership exist, developing generative learning for adaptability and agility in a school requires a different set of mindsets and skills.

An essential feature of leadership in this model is distributed leadership, which points to developing other leaders to run successful learning teams. A second essential feature is that this model's mindsets and skills focus around creating interdependence at the individual, group, and system level. A third essential feature is that these mindsets and skills happen within the broader processes similar to the routines explained in each preceding chapter supported by cross-cutting themes of generating learning, building knowledge, and requiring relational skills.

These mindsets and skills focus on developing the conditions and processes for learning at the individual, team, and organizational levels. These skills do not consider all of the other abilities good school leaders need to efficiently manage their buildings. Instead, they point out newer mindsets and skills that emerge when they begin to install a new operating system. As Heifetz and Linsky (2002) point out, in this new world of complexity, we can no longer use technical strategies (things we know how to do), but instead, we must employ adaptive strategies. In other words,

Capacity Model Area	Leadership Mindsets	Leadership Skill(s)
Capacity as Organizational Conditions	• Creating the right conditions for growth • Distributing leadership	1. Developing positivity. 2. Strategizing, focusing and prioritizing. 3. Crafting purpose with a clear theory of action. 4. Managing knowledge. 5. Developing leadership teams and collaboration. 6. Building collective responsibility. 7. Managing knowledge.
Capacity as Organizational Processes 1. Information foraging	• Future oriented • Growth mindset	1. Scanning the environment. 2. Initiating and cultivating engagement. 3. Seeing connections among systems. 4. Jointly determining problems and needs. 5. Developing team processing.
2. Intuiting (individual learning)	• Recognizing insights • Growth mindset	1. Working with beliefs and clarifying mental models. 2. Leading systematic processing. 3. Influencing efficacy. 4. Noticing hidden patterns.
3. Interpreting (individual and team learning)	• Crafting meaning • Growth mindset	1. Developing and analyzing teaming and using learning processes. 2. Creating psychological safety. 3. Influencing collective efficacy. 4. Building short inquiry cycles and narrowing to action. 5. Developing team processing.

Figure 8.2 Leaders' New Mindsets and Skills

Capacity Model Area	Leadership Mindsets	Leadership Skill(s)
4. Integrating (individual and team learning)	• Creating feedback loops for adaptability • Growth mindset	1. Helping others design and build ideas and running inquiry cycles. 2. Fostering disciplined inquiry and understanding impact. 3. Helping others learn from their actions/reinforcing. 4. Reframing connections and integrating ideas. 5. Helping others stay open.
5. Institutionalizing (organizational learning)	• Crafting coherence and accountability • Growth mindset	1. Building precise language and a common knowledge base. 2. Sustaining focus. 3. Amplifying success and deviance and moving toward precision. 4. Unifying
Cross-cutting themes	• Generating learning • Building knowledge • Going deeper	1. Communicating explicitly and challenging the status quo. 2. Building curiosity in others and developing clear theories of action. 3. Developing team processes. 4. Building relationships and trust. 5. Connecting people and creating networks. 6. Learning alongside and building personal knowledge. 7. Seeing the system, the details and their interconnections.

Figure 8.2 (Cont.)

learning through the challenge in which "people with the problem must be part and parcel of the solution" (Fullan, 2019). These adaptive challenges require new learning processes and new skills for the leader(s).

The overarching metaphor for formal leadership in this model could be coder, given the focus on developing a new operating system for schools. However, we think that a conductor is a more appropriate metaphor to convey. Fullan (2019) described this type of leader when he stated that nuanced leaders,

> Have a curiosity about what is possible, openness to other people, sensitivity to context, and loyalty to a better future. They see below the surface, enabling them to detect patterns and the consequences for the system. They connect people to their own and each others' humanity. They don't lead; they teach. They change people's emotions, not just their minds. They have an instinct for orchestration …

A conductor's role is to bring all of the diverse instruments, skills, beliefs, and talents together to produce engaging and beautiful music. While the conductor moves the whole orchestra in one way, leads in sections develop the other musicians while the conductor focuses on the leads.

Similarly, while the conductor probably cannot play all of the instruments, they understand music and how best to integrate various styles into a coherent sound. Conductors understand each musician, their temperaments, their beliefs, and their motivations toward a common purpose of creating a beautiful sound. In other words, the conductor/leader needs to understand learning at levels.

Final Thoughts

Rudi Dornbusch was a famous German economist who famously wrote about economic catastrophes: "Crises take longer to arrive than you can possibly imagine, but when they do come, they happen faster than you can possibly imagine."

This statement is true in economics and now education. The problems of the past have been elevated through the current set of crises leading to high degrees of uncertainty. With growing inequality, climate change, and workforce changes, people, including students, feel uneasy and uncomfortable about the future. We have seen crisis after crisis play out and our school leaders and teachers taking heroic actions to continue to educate the next generation. What were once stable institutions and patterns for our lives have become upended leading to a foregone conclusion. Different skills and forms of education are now more necessary than ever to prepare students to prosper in these new, complex contexts and the dizzying rate of change they will face.

Think about it this way. Primary-aged students will not graduate high school until the 2030's by which time technology will have more than likely morphed into something we cannot even conceive today. As Yorks and Nicolaides (2013) explained:

> One effect of this intensifying pace of technological innovation has been the increasingly dynamic complexity of the systems in which people are embedded: systemic and interpersonal networks consisting of conflict, interdependence, ambiguity, and flux. By the end of the first decade of the 21st century, the increasing pace of change and the complexity of connections it brings with it has become a continuous reality in the lives of citizens.

Similarly, to describe the times in which we now live, Nicolaides (2015) suggested:

> The metaphor of liquidity effectively captures the complexity of the social changes taking place in everyday life. Increasingly, social structures widely viewed as solid—education, health, social security, leisure, and family, to name only a few—are more fluid, unable to hold their shape for long. This new liquidity signals constant change, and with it insecurity and uncertainty: about what to wear, who to follow, what matters, and what to learn. Individuals worldwide appear increasingly insecure about how best to go about the business of their everyday lives, evidenced by the changing face of higher education and labor force demands.

We believe that more generative forms of learning and knowledge building are the only ways that we can again find solid ground in these waves of liquidity. Only by working through these problems and collectively learning from our actions can we continue to keep our heads above water. Schools and those who lead have a unique role in these times. They must not only understand and try and predict the future their students will engage in, but they must also create new ways of working and learning for the adults in their organizations. Leaders in all forms must develop places where learning is an ongoing and inevitable role for all. We hope this new model for integrating individual, team, and organizational learning to develop enhanced capacity and knowledge building for the future is a step toward this ideal. Our students are depending on us.

References

Bereiter, C. and Scardamalia, M.(2014). Knowledge building and knowledge creation: One concept, two hills to climb. In S. C. Tan, H. J. So, J. Yeo (eds) *Knowledge creation in education* (35–52). Springer.

Corbin, J. (2017). *Surprising results from the 2017 Gallup employee engagement survey.* www.theemployeeapp.com/gallup-2017-employee-engagement-report-results-nothing-changed/

Della Corte, V. and Del Gaudio, G. (2012). Dynamic capabilities: A still unexplored issue with growing complexity. *Corporate Ownership & Control,* 9 (4), 327–338.

Ford, M. (2013). https://phys.org/news/2013-01-future-machines-jobs.html

Friedman, T. (2016). *Thank you for being late: An optimist's guide to thriving in the age of accelerations.* Strauss & Giroux.

Fullan, M. (2011). *Learning is the Work.* [Unpublished manuscript]. http://michaelfullan.ca/wp-content/uploads/2016/06/13396087260.pdf

Fullan, M. (2019). *Nuance: Why some leaders succeed and others fail.* Corwin.

Heifetz, R.A. and Linksky, M. (2002). *Leadership on the line: Staying alive through the dangers of leading.* Harvard Business School Press.

Katz, L.F. and Krueger, A.B. (2016). The rise and nature of alternative work arrangements in the US, 1195–2015. https://krueger.princeton.edu/sites/default/files/akrueger/files/katz_krueger_cws_-_march_29_20165.pdf

Kauffman Foundation (2019). *Visions of the future: Ewing Marion Kauffman Foundation Research Findings.* www.kauffman.org/-/media/kauffman_org/currents-redesign/2019/09/kauffman-visions-of-the-future-research-results-9162019.pdf?la=en

McGowan, H. and Shipley, C. (2017). *Preparing students to lose their jobs*. www.linkedin.com/pulse/preparing-students-lose-jobs-heather-mcgowan/

McGowan, H. and Shipley, C. (2020). *The adaptation advantage: Let go, learn fast, and thrive in the future of work*. Wiley.

NGLC Framework. https://myways.nextgenlearning.org/

Nicolaïtes, A. (2015). Generative learning: Adults learning with ambiguity. *Adult Education Quarterly 2015,* 65 (3), 179–195; doi: 10.1177/0741713614568887

Rohanna, K. (2018). *Preparing schools to successfully participate in networked improvement communities: A case study of year 1 of a math instructional network*. Unpublished doctoral dissertation. University of California, Los Angeles.

The Agile Mindset: Futureproofing Students (2017). www.becker.edu/wp-content/uploads/2018/08/The-Agile-Mindset.pdf

Vera, D., Crossan, M. and Apaydin, M. (2011). A framework for integrating organizational learning, knowledge, capabilities, and absorptive capacity. In Easterby-Smith, M., Lyles, M., (eds), *Handbook of organizational learning and knowledge management*, (2nd edn, 153–180). Wiley.

Yorks, L. and Nicolaides, A. (2013). *Toward an integral approach for evolving mindsets for generative learning and timely action in the midst of ambiguity*. Teachers College Press. 115.

Appendix A
Diagnostic for School Learning Capacity

Directions: This diagnostic can be used in two separate ways: (1) after each chapter, your leadership team or staff can take the diagnostic and aggregate the results to look for areas of strength and areas in need of improvement, or (2) your leadership team and staff can take the entire diagnostic at once and aggregate the results to look for areas of strength and areas in need of improvement. In addition, the entire diagnostic can be given to your entire staff for perceptions about capacity at all three levels of learning.

The diagnostic is based on the overall capacity model outlined in Chapters 1–6.

Levels of Learning	Relation to 5i Model	Systems and elements to help develop learning capacity
1. Organizational Learning	Information Foraging Institutionalizing	*Organizational conditions* (a) Clarity of purpose and instructional guidance (b) Coherence (c) Distributed leadership (d) Positive culture (e) Learning agility *Organizational processes* (a) 5i model (b) Improvement and innovation

Appendix A

Levels of Learning	Relation to 5i Model	Systems and elements to help develop learning capacity
2. Individual learning	Intuiting integrating	(a) Expertise and deliberate practice (b) Beliefs and mental models (c) Self-efficacy (d) Conceptual change models
3. Team learning	Integrating institutionalizing	(a) Teaming (b) Team learning (c) Psychological safety (d) Collective efficacy

Organizational Conditions: The school develops and uses conditions to support ongoing learning about external demands and areas for internal improvement.

Conditions at this level of learning	Diagnostic questions	Responses 1. Highly inaccurate 2. Somewhat in accurate 3. Not sure 4. Somewhat accurate 5. Highly accurate				
1. Clarity of purpose and instructional guidance	1a. Our purpose as a school gives us clear direction for coordination	1	2	3	4	5
	1b. Our school has well defined instructional guidance plans	1	2	3	4	5
	1c. Our improvement or innovation goals have a clear purpose	1	2	3	4	5
	1d. Each area or domain that we teach has a clear vision of success	1	2	3	4	5
	1e. Our school has a strong sense of press for academics and other important outcomes	1	2	3	4	5
		Total ___/5=				

Appendix A

Conditions at this level of learning	Diagnostic questions	Responses
2. Coherence	2a. We coordinate our learning around a clear direction for improvement.	1 2 3 4 5
	2b. We coordinate our team learning around a clear direction for improvement.	1 2 3 4 5
	2c. Our improvement work has a clear purpose to it	1 2 3 4 5
	2d. Our school aligns its resources with our improvement efforts	1 2 3 4 5
	2e. Teachers develop similar beliefs around our improvement efforts	1 2 3 4 5
		Total ____/5=
3. Distributed leadership	3a. Our leadership communicates clear direction for learning	1 2 3 4 5
	3b. Leadership for learning or improvement is shared between principals, teachers and others	1 2 3 4 5
	3c Other staff members are well prepared to lead learning	1 2 3 4 5
	3d. Others influence me beyond formal leaders	1 2 3 4 5
	3e. Staff member are consistently involved in making decisions about improvement	1 2 3 4 5
		Total ____/5=
4. Positive culture	4a. Communication systems promote a flow of information across the entire school	1 2 3 4 5
	4b. The people in our school show compassion toward one another	1 2 3 4 5

Appendix A

Conditions at this level of learning	Diagnostic questions	Responses
	4c. The people in our school are forgiving.	1 2 3 4 5
	4d. The people in our school express gratitude to one another	1 2 3 4 5
	4e. The people in our school have rich relationships with one another	1 2 3 4 5
	4f. The people in our school are very giving to one another	1 2 3 4 5
	4g. The people in our school communicate with lots of affirmation.	1 2 3 4 5
	4h. The people in our school communicate with supportive language	1 2 3 4 5
	4i. Our school feels like it is pursuing a profound vision for our students' futures	1 2 3 4 5
	4j. I feel like we are having a positive impact on students and each other	1 2 3 4 5
	4k. My work has personal meaning to me	1 2 3 4 5
	4l. Our school feels like it has lots of positive energy	1 2 3 4 5
	4m. Our school feels like it directs our discretional energy in the right ways	1 2 3 4 5
	4n. In our school people show up with lots of energy	1 2 3 4 5
		Total ___/14=

Appendix A

Conditions at this level of learning	Diagnostic questions	Responses
5. Learning agility • **absorptive capacity** • **dynamic capability** • **knowledge management**	5a. Our school is good at determining if external ideas could add value to our students	1 2 3 4 5
	5b. Our school is good at understanding new ideas coming from the external environment	1 2 3 4 5
	5c. Our school has a strong ability to develop a shared understanding of new ideas	1 2 3 4 5
	5d. Once our school accepts an idea, the idea quickly becomes something we use.	1 2 3 4 5
	5e. Once our school accepts an idea, we quickly generate new knowledge from using it.	1 2 3 4 5
	5f. Teachers at our school are good at sharing their deep knowledge of teaching and learning with others	1 2 3 4 5
	5g. We have a common technological system to store and retrieve knowledge and products.	1 2 3 4 5
		Total ____/7 =

Appendix A

Organizational Learning Processes: The school develops and uses organizational processes to support ongoing learning about external demands and areas for internal improvement.

Processes at this level of learning	Diagnostic questions	Responses
		1. Highly inaccurate
		2. Somewhat in accurate
		3. Not sure
		4. Somewhat accurate
		5. Highly accurate
1. 5i organizational learning process	1a. Our school has a method to scan the external environment for ideas that will help our school	1 2 3 4 5
	1b. When considering new ideas, our school allows us time to generate insights and patterns	1 2 3 4 5
	1c. When considering new ideas, we create shared mental models together	1 2 3 4 5
	1d. When considering new ideas our team/school develops coordinated actions to try them out	1 2 3 4 5
	1e. When considering new ideas our team/school uses cycles to refine the idea	1 2 3 4 5
	1f. Many of the new ideas we have considered become common routines or processes in our school.	1 2 3 4 5
	1g. When trying new ideas, we often generate new knowledge about the idea.	1 2 3 4 5
		Total ____/7=

Appendix A

Processes at this level of learning	Diagnostic questions	Responses				
2. Special learning processes	2a. Our school often uses cycles of inquiry to generate new learnings about a problem of learning	1	2	3	4	5
	2b. Our school uses different learning methods for new innovative ideas versus improving what we already do.	1	2	3	4	5
	2c. We often iterate on ideas to make them work for our students	1	2	3	4	5
	2d. In our learning processes we often collect various forms of data	1	2	3	4	5
	2e. We often consider the needs of our students when designing new trials	1	2	3	4	5
	2f. We often generate new insights during our cycles of learning	1	2	3	4	5
	2g. We often use a common design process to solve common problems of practice.	1	2	3	4	5

Total ____/7=

Individual Learning Level: The school develops the necessary elements and routines to support ongoing individual learning about external demands and areas for internal improvement.

Processes and supports at this level of learning	Diagnostic questions	Responses
		1. Highly inaccurate
		2. Somewhat in accurate
		3. Not sure
		4. Somewhat accurate
		5. Highly accurate

Appendix A

Processes and supports at this level of learning	Diagnostic questions	Responses
1. Expertise and deliberate practice	1a. Our school has an explicit way to determine expertise with new ideas or innovations	1　2　3　4　5
	1b. Our school has an explicit way to determine if people are plateauing in their growth around new ideas or techniques	1　2　3　4　5
	1c. Our school has a process to create deliberate practice for teachers around new ideas or innovations	1　2　3　4　5
	1d. Our school has explicit ways to support the growth of individuals toward expertise.	1　2　3　4　5 Total ____/4=
2. Beliefs and mental models	2a. Our school has explicitly addressed the roles of beliefs in teaching and learning.	1　2　3　4　5
	2b. Our school develops the beliefs about new ideas and shares these with teachers.	1　2　3　4　5
	2c. Our school frequently addresses beliefs about new ideas during learning phases.	1　2　3　4　5
	2d. Individuals and teams recognize their biases when learning about new ideas.	1　2　3　4　5 Total ____/4=

Appendix A

Processes and supports at this level of learning	Diagnostic questions	Responses
3. Self-efficacy	3a. Our school explicitly addresses the role of self-efficacy in addressing new ideas.	1 2 3 4 5
	3b. When developing learning opportunities our school considers various ways to develop self-efficacy.	1 2 3 4 5
	3c. During learning and change efforts, our school tries to determine levels of self-efficacy.	1 2 3 4 5
	3d. Our leaders try to intervene when low self-efficacy is evident in teachers.	1 2 3 4 5
		Total ____/4=
4. Conceptual change models	4a. Our school uses a specific conceptual change model when introducing new ideas.	1 2 3 4 5
	4b. At our school new ideas are presented with enough detail for teachers to process.	1 2 3 4 5
	4c. Our school uses a systematic processing method to help teachers compare the new idea to their current practice.	1 2 3 4 5
	4d. Our school is good at recognizing the affective dimension of accepting new ideas.	1 2 3 4 5
		Total ____/4=

Appendix A

Team Learning Level: The school develops the necessary elements and routines to support ongoing team learning about external demands and areas for internal improvement.

Processes and supports at this level of learning	Diagnostic questions	Responses 1. Highly inaccurate 2. Somewhat in accurate 3. Not sure 4. Somewhat accurate 5. Highly accurate				
1. Teaming	1a. At our school we use both short-term and long-term teams for much of our work	1	2	3	4	5
	1b. At our school our teams spend time on the affective dimensions of working together	1	2	3	4	5
	1c. At our school our teams typically collect, share and analyze information together.	1	2	3	4	5
	1d. At our school our teams are responsive to the needs of all of our students.	1	2	3	4	5
		Total ____/4=				
2. Learning in teams	2a. In our team(s) we use processes for collective inquiry around common problems of practice	1	2	3	4	5
	2b. In our team(s) we use joint work to learn from our actions	1	2	3	4	5

Appendix A

Processes and supports at this level of learning	Diagnostic questions	Responses
	2c. In our team(s) we believe that we are interdependent	1 2 3 4 5
	2d. In our team we use representation practices (collective lesson planning, student work, replaying and rehearsal etc.)	1 2 3 4 5
	2e. In our team(s) we frame learning problems around both teaching and learning issues.	1 2 3 4 5
	2f. In our team(s) we believe we can learn collectively from our actions.	1 2 3 4 5
	2g. In our team(s) we take time to learn from our failures.	1 2 3 4 5 Total ____/7=
3. Psychological safety	3a. People on my team are eager to share information about what does and does not work.	1 2 3 4 5
	3b. Making mistakes is considered part of the learning process on our teams	1 2 3 4 5
	3c. If I make a mistake on my team, it will not be held against me.	1 2 3 4 5
	3d. On my team, teaches feel comfortable experimenting with untried teaching approaches, even if the approach might not work.	1 2 3 4 5

Appendix A

Processes and supports at this level of learning	Diagnostic questions	Responses
	3e. On my team, it is easy to speak up about what is on your mind.	1 2 3 4 5
	3f. People on my team are usually comfortable talking about problems and disagreements about teaching and learning.	1 2 3 4 5 Total ___/6=
4. Collective efficacy	4a. Teachers on my team are confident they will be able to motivate their students	1 2 3 4 5
	4b. Teachers on my team have the skills need to produce meaningful student learning	1 2 3 4 5
	4c. If a child doesn't learn something, teachers on my team will try another way.	1 2 3 4 5
	4d. Teachers on my team believe that every child can learn	1 2 3 4 5
	4e. Teachers on my team are skilled in various methods of teaching	1 2 3 4 5
	4f. On my team teachers have what it takes to explore new instructional approaches to help underperforming students.	1 2 3 4 5 Total ___/6=